PERCEIVE CHUCHU

AI Explorers

Minds Among Machines

First published by Perceive Chuchu, Pretoria, South Africa 2026

First edition

ISBN: 978-1-04-927323-5

This book was professionally typeset on Reedsy.
Find out more at reedsy.com

Contents

Preface

Artificial intelligence may be something you have heard about in conferences, documentaries, and science fiction films. Today, it sits quietly in your pocket, shapes your search results, improves your photos, guides your work, and, if you are reading this book, has probably already changed how you think about the future.

For decades, the world viewed AI through two extremes: either as a magical superpower or a mysterious threat. Neither view helps the everyday professional, parent, student, or leader who desires to understand what AI means for their life. Which skills will remain important? What opportunities are opening up? How should these tools be used responsibly?

This book answers those questions with clarity, confidence, and warmth. It will not overwhelm you with mathematics or jargon, nor does it assume you are a programmer or engineer. It asks only one thing: curiosity.

AI Explorers: *Minds Among Machines* is a guide for our time. It invites you to understand how artificial intelligence really works, how it fits into your work and daily life, and how to use it wisely and creatively. Whether you are an executive preparing for a transformed workplace, a lifelong learner curious about the next decade, or a technical beginner wanting an intelligent overview, this book offers a path forward.

Most importantly, this book reminds us that AI is not simply about machines; it is about us, our values, our decisions, and the future we choose to create.

If this book is in your hands, you are already an explorer.

Let the journey begin.

— Perceive Chuchu

Introduction

Why This Book Exists

There has never been a better or more overwhelming time to learn about AI. New tools appear weekly. Jobs evolve. Entire industries shift. Everyone is asking the same questions:

- What exactly is AI?
- How does it work?
- What does it mean for my job?
- Will it replace me or empower me?
- How can I use it today, not someday?

You are not alone. The world is learning together, and most people feel behind—even the experts.

This book is designed to change that.

What You Will Get From This Book

By the time you finish, you will:

- Clearly understand how modern AI works
- Know how to use AI tools in your personal and professional life
- See how AI is transforming industries
- Understand its risks and limitations

- Develop AI-enhanced thinking skills
- Know how to future-proof your career
- Feel confident, not confused

This Is Not A Textbook

It is not a collection of technical papers. It is a guide for real people living in a real world shaped by powerful technology.

How to Read This Book

You do not need any programming background. No mathematics. No engineering degree. Just curiosity.

Each chapter is intentionally concise, clear, lived-in, and practical. Some chapters will help you use AI immediately. Others will reshape how you think about work, society, and the mind. You will find diagrams, examples, stories, workflows, and try-it-yourself moments.

You can read this book in any order, but starting from the beginning builds a foundation that makes everything else clearer.

Why AI Matters Now

AI is not just a technology story. It is a human story. It is changing how we learn, create, communicate, work, and make decisions. It is a tool, a partner, a mirror, and sometimes a challenge. The people who thrive in the next decade will not be the ones who know *everything* about AI—they will be the ones who know how to *adapt*. This book will help you do exactly that.

Welcome to AI Explorers. Let us understand Minds and Machines together.

I

PART 1—Understanding AI: The Foundations

AI can feel mysterious, overwhelming, or intimidating—but it does not have to be. Part 1 clears the myths, offering a simple and accurate foundation. By the end of this section, you will understand what AI truly is, what it is not, and how it applies to the world around you.

1

A Short Story: Before the Fog Lifted

Charlize first noticed the contradiction on a quiet Sunday morning.

An article on her phone declared that artificial intelligence was about to change everything; another warned that the transformation was already underway, while a third dismissed it as mostly hype—all spoken with confidence, yet each telling a different story.

She had heard the term AI for years, but lately it seemed to be everywhere, woven into conversations about work, education, creativity, and even ethics. People spoke of it as though it were one coherent force—a tool in some moments, a threat in others, and perhaps even an intelligence waiting to emerge.

What unsettled her was not fear, but confusion.

AI was described as intelligent, yet it did not seem to understand—powerful, yet strangely limited; new, yet apparently decades old. Some claimed it could do almost anything, while others insisted it barely did anything at all.

She began to wonder whether the problem was not AI itself, but rather the way it was discussed.

Her thoughts drifted back to earlier technologies she had lived through. Computers once filled entire rooms. The internet began as a curiosity. Smartphones were dismissed as unnecessary. Each time, the story people told mattered as much as the technology itself.

So she started asking quieter questions.

When did AI actually begin? Was it always about learning machines, or had it worked differently at one point? Why did some systems follow rules, while others learned from examples? What did people really mean when they spoke about levels of intelligence? And why did modern AI feel astonishingly capable in some areas, yet completely fail in others?

As she paid closer attention, patterns began to emerge.

Older systems behaved predictably, almost mechanically, while newer ones adapted. Some produced answers; others generated content. None appeared aware. None had goals of their own. And yet, together, they quietly shaped decisions, recommendations, and outcomes in subtle but meaningful ways.

AI, she realised, was not a single invention. It was a progression.

A layering of ideas over time—rules giving way to learning, learning giving way to models that captured structure, relationships, and probability. Systems built from data, trained through repetition, and applied within carefully defined boundaries.

That realisation changed everything.

AI stopped feeling like an unknowable force and began to look like engineering: clever, imperfect, and constrained. It became clear why it excelled at recognising patterns, predicting outcomes, and generating responses, yet struggled with judgement, context, and meaning.

The mystery did not disappear, but it became manageable.

Charlize understood why AI could assist but not replace, suggest but not decide, accelerate work but not absolve responsibility. Its strengths were real—and so were its limits.

And once she saw AI for what it truly was—not magic, not consciousness, but systems built from methods and models—the fog finally began to lift.

What lay ahead was no longer speculation about the future; it was understanding what was already here.

> *This fictional story introduces the themes of* ***Part 1****.*

2

What AI Really Is and What It Is Not

Most people misunderstand artificial intelligence—not for its complexity, but for the overly technical and intimidating way it is often explained. For decades, AI lived in research labs, science fiction movies, and conference presentations packed with equations. For the everyday professional, AI felt distant, mystical, or even threatening. Then, almost overnight, AI became personal.

It started writing emails, summarising documents, generating images, helping children study, and assisting doctors, lawyers, designers, and entrepreneurs. The world suddenly woke up to a single, surprising truth: *AI is not a far-off future. AI is now*. However, before we can use it confidently, we must understand something deeper: what AI actually *is*, and what it *is not*.

This chapter is your foundation. Once you grasp these core ideas, everything else in this book will feel easier, clearer, and more intuitive.

The Definition You Will Remember

If you search the internet for "What is AI?", you will get definitions filled with words like *algorithms*, *neural networks*, and *autonomous systems*. None of those helps if you are trying to understand the essence.

It is helpful to start by defining what data actually is and where it comes from, especially if you are new to the topic. *Data* is information collected from real-world and digital activities. It can originate from many sources—text we type, messages we send, photos we capture, sensors in devices, websites we browse, and even the everyday actions that computers measure.

Here is a simple and accurate definition of what AI is:

> *Artificial Intelligence is a system that learns patterns from data and uses them to make predictions or create content.*

Give an AI millions of images of cats, and it learns what cat patterns look like.

Give it billions of sentences, and it learns language patterns.

Give it financial data, and it learns economic patterns.

AI does not "know" in the same way humans do. Instead, it *recognises patterns* and uses them to guess what comes next. This simple concept explains everything modern AI does.

Why AI Feels Human, Even When It Is Not

If AI is just pattern recognition, why does it feel so human? How can it:

- answer questions with confidence,
- write essays that sound polished,
- have conversations,
- write code,
- summarise reports,
- and even offer advice?

This is because language—the way we speak, write, and communicate is deeply patterned: structure, grammar, tone, style, word choice, logic, rhythm, and emotional cues.

AI models are trained on massive amounts of text to learn these patterns in breathtaking detail. So when you ask an AI tool a question, it is not "thinking" the way humans do. It is doing something more mechanical, yet powerful: *predicting the next most likely, coherent, and useful pattern of words.*

In humans, we refer to this as intelligence—in AI, it's statistics at scale. When you understand this distinction, AI becomes less frightening and more empowering.

What AI Is Not

Let's clear up some of the common misconceptions.

- AI is not conscious—it has no desires, dreams, emotions, or inner life.
- AI is not self-aware—it does not know it exists. Neither does it "understand" its answers.
- AI is not a human brain—it does not learn the way you learned to read, drive, or solve problems.
- AI is not perfect—it can make mistakes—sometimes confidently.
- AI is not magic—it cannot solve every problem. It also cannot fix broken systems or replace human judgement.
- AI is not a threat by default—like any tool, it depends on how people choose to use it.

Understanding what AI *is not* helps avoid two traps: fear and over-trusting.

A Better Way to Think About AI

Here is a metaphor that will serve you throughout this book:

> *AI is like a powerful autocomplete engine.*

When you type a message, and your phone predicts the next word, that is autocomplete. Modern AI is an autocomplete system for language, images, audio, video, code, and charts.

This is why AI can:

- finish your sentences
- generate realistic images
- write business proposals
- plan a schedule
- debug code
- create presentations
- summarise a meeting
- analyse financial statements

It has seen patterns before, and your request activates the closest patterns in its training. It then predicts a coherent output. This framing helps you stay realistic about what AI can and cannot do.

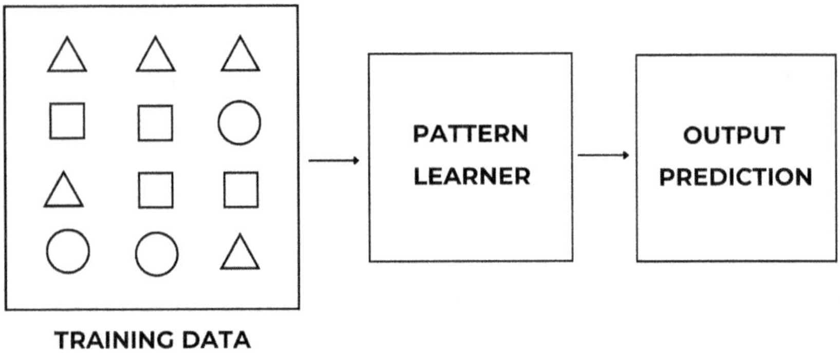

***Figure 1.1**: How AI learns by analysing many examples to discover patterns and make predictions.*

Why AI Sometimes "Hallucinates"

One of the strangest behaviours of AI is that it sometimes gives answers that are wrong, half-true, confidently inaccurate, or completely invented. These are called *hallucinations*. Why does this happen? Because AI does not verify facts, but it predicts patterns. If a pattern appears frequently in its training data, AI may produce it even if it is wrong. If you ask a question AI has no real reference for, it may generate something that *sounds right* but is not.

Understanding the following helps you use AI more wisely:

- Always sanity-check important information.
- Ask AI to provide sources or cross-checks.
- Ask for multiple possibilities, not one answer.
- Use iterative prompting ("Let us think step-by-step...") to reduce risk.

This does not make AI bad; it makes AI predictable once you know the rules.

What AI Can Do Today

AI can:

- summarise complex information
- generate text, designs, and code
- analyse data patterns
- help with decision-making
- automate repetitive tasks
- enhance creativity
- improve productivity dramatically
- make learning faster
- act as a thinking partner

Every chapter in this book will show practical examples you can apply immediately.

ABILITY	HUMANS	AI
CONTEXT	Excellent	Limited
SPEED	Slower	Fast
PATTERN MEMORY	Good	Massive
UNDERSTANDING	Real	None

***Figure 1.2**: Human and AI strengths shown side by side.*

What AI Cannot Do Yet

AI cannot:

- understand context the way humans do
- think in long-term goals
- make independent decisions
- replace human emotions, ethics, or empathy
- fully grasp real-world experience
- reason about physical environments reliably
- innovate without human direction

AI is not a replacement for human intelligence, but it is an amplifier.

The Human-AI Partnership Begins Here

The most important idea in this book is this:

> *AI does its best work when paired with human judgement and creativity.*

You bring: context, ethics, lived experience, intuition, big-picture thinking, originality

AI brings: speed, scale, pattern recognition, tireless repetition, instant generation, data-driven predictions

Together, you form a partnership that is more powerful than ever before. Every chapter from here on will show you how to build that partnership in your work, career, industry, and personal life.

A Simple Exercise

Ask an AI tool the following questions in sequence:

1. "Explain artificial intelligence to me as if I'm 12 years old."
2. "Explain artificial intelligence to me as if I'm a CEO."

Notice how the explanation changes. Notice the patterns, the strengths, and the gaps. This small exercise will show you more about AI in 30 seconds than any technical article ever could.

The two questions we have just asked the AI tool are *prompts.* Writing of prompts is what we call *prompting*, and *prompt engineering* is the practice of learning how to create effective prompts.

* * *

Summary:

- AI is pattern recognition at scale.
- It is not conscious, magical, or human-like.
- It generates human-like output because language is patterned.
- It can hallucinate because it predicts, but does not verify.
- AI is powerful but limited.
- Those who collaborate with AI will have a distinct advantage over those who resist it.

3

A Short, Fascinating History of AI

Artificial intelligence feels modern, and it shows up in our phones, workplaces, search engines, and in our conversations. The story of AI did not begin with smartphones, chatbots, or algorithms, but it began with a simple, timeless question: *Can a machine think?*

For decades, that question drove scientists, philosophers, engineers, and dreamers. The path that led to today's generative AI is full of breakthroughs, failures, and sudden leaps forward that no one saw coming. Understanding this journey will help you see why AI works the way it does today, and where it might be heading next.

This is the story of how we got here:

1. The Idea Before the Technology (1950s)

Long before AI existed, the idea existed.

Alan Turing: The Spark That Started It All

In 1950, Alan Turing, a British mathematician and computer scientist, asked a bold and unsettling question: *"Can machines think?"*

He proposed the *Turing Test*, a simple idea: if a machine can hold a conversation so convincingly that a human cannot distinguish it from a person, should we call that intelligence? At the time, computers were "room-sized calculators." Yet Turing saw beyond the hardware—he saw possibility. This single idea planted the seed for everything AI would become.

Figure 2.1: *A symbolic illustration of the Turing Test, in which a judge decides whether responses come from a human or a machine.*

2. The Birth of AI as a Field (1956)

The term *Artificial Intelligence* was coined by John McCarthy, an American computer scientist, in 1956 at the Dartmouth Conference. This is often considered the AI's official birthday. A group of researchers gathered to explore a daring hypothesis:

> *"Every aspect of learning or intelligence can, in principle, be described so precisely that a machine can be made to simulate it."*

These early pioneers believed machines could eventually reason, learn, and solve problems. Their confidence set the tone for decades.

3. The First Approaches: Rules, Logic, and Symbolic AI (1960s–1980s)

Before data-driven AI, there was *Symbolic AI*; systems built on rules written by humans. For many decades, it dominated the field. Humans defined the rules, and machines executed them exactly. This is also known as *Classical AI*.

If X happens, then do Y.
If this condition is true, make that decision.

Symbolic AI is narrow by design. It performs well in controlled environments with clear logic but struggles as complexity, ambiguity, or variability increase. As a result, it could not scale to complex, real-world problems such as language, vision, or open-ended decision-making.

Although it is no longer the dominant approach to AI, Symbolic AI has not disappeared; it remains effective in domains where rules are stable and outcomes must be predictable.

Areas where Symbolic AI still shines include:

- tax and compliance systems
- medical coding and classification
- expert systems in finance and law
- industrial automation with predictable conditions
- rule-based components of games like chess

Symbolic AI is reliable because humans write the rules. However, it breaks down when situations do not follow clear logic, such as natural conversation or uncertain environments.

Symbolic AI had potential, but it did not scale. Human intelligence could not be reduced to a massive rulebook.

4. The Statistical Machine Learning Revolution (1990s)

Instead of programming rules manually, scientists explored a new idea: *what if machines could learn rules from data on their own?*

This shift from "tell the machine what to do" to "let the machine learn" changed everything. Machine learning allowed computers to recognise patterns in data, such as:

- detecting spam emails
- recognising handwriting
- predicting simple outcomes

The results were humble but powerful. For the first time, machines improved with experience. Something bigger was on the horizon.

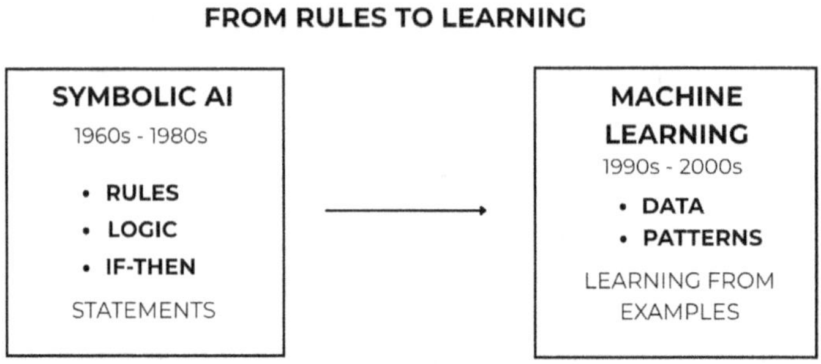

***Figure** 2.2: How AI shifted from hand-crafted rules to systems that learn patterns from data.*

5. The Deep Learning Explosion (2012)

A breakthrough moment arrived in 2012, when *deep neural networks*—AI systems inspired by the brain—began to succeed at scale. This breakthrough was exemplified by the neural network *AlexNet*, which outperformed all competitors in an image-recognition competition. This single event reshaped the field overnight because it proved that when models (*think of a model as the 'brain' of the AI system; the part that has learned patterns from data and can now produce answers*) grow large enough and data becomes abundant:

- machines can discover patterns humans cannot see
- accuracy skyrockets
- learning becomes more fluid
- new possibilities emerge rapidly

This was the moment deep learning moved from research labs into industry—and from then on, the world was not quite the same.

6. The Transformer Revolution (2017)

If deep learning sparked progress, the *Transformer architecture* ignited a revolution. Introduced by researchers at Google in 2017, Transformers introduced a powerful concept called *attention*—a mechanism that enables AI to focus on the most relevant parts of data. For language, this was transformative. Suddenly, AI could understand relationships across long sentences, paragraphs, and pages. Transformers paved the way for GPT models, chatbots, image generation, translation systems and modern generative AI. This was the turning point that made today's AI possible.

7. The Generative AI Wave (2022–2025)

Then came the moment most people noticed AI in their own lives. In late 2022, ChatGPT was released, making AI conversational, responsive, accessible, and useful.

For the first time, AI felt less like a tool and more like a partner. Suddenly, it was used by:

- students to study
- professionals to write emails and brainstorm
- businesses to innovate
- artists to create
- developers to write code
- individuals to enhance everyday life

Generative AI changed public perception. AI moved from labs and servers into daily human interaction.

8. The Human-AI Era

Today, we live in a world where:

- Humans provide context, ethics, and creativity
- AI provides speed, memory, and pattern recognition

This partnership marks a new stage of intelligence: distributed intelligence, where human and machine strengths complement each other. We are, in every sense, *minds among machines*. And while AI has advanced rapidly, the greatest impact still lies ahead. Understanding the journey helps you understand the future and your place in it.

* * *

Summary:

- The idea of AI began as a philosophical question.
- Early AI relied on rules and logic, but struggled with complex problems.
- Machine learning introduced data-driven learning.
- Deep learning and neural networks unlocked modern capabilities.
- Transformers revolutionised language understanding.
- Generative AI brought AI into everyday life.
- We are now in an era of human–AI partnership.

4

Levels of AI

Before exploring how AI works or where it is used, we need to clear up one of the most common sources of confusion: AI is discussed at different levels of capability.

When people argue about AI, they are often talking past each other. Some are describing systems that exist today. Others are imagining systems that do not yet exist. To avoid confusion, it helps to distinguish between three broad levels of AI.

Artificial Narrow Intelligence (ANI)

Artificial Narrow Intelligence, known as *Narrow AI*, refers to AI systems designed to perform specific tasks. This is the most common type of AI, and probably the only one you have used until very recently. This type of AI cannot generalise beyond its purpose. It cannot think or decide what it wants to do next.

Examples of narrow AI you use every day—often without noticing:

- Google Maps finds the fastest route
- Netflix recommends what to watch next

- Banking apps flag fraudulent transactions
- Email systems filter spam
- Autocorrect completes sentences
- Digital cameras detect faces

These systems do not understand what they are doing; they are just extremely good at the patterns they were trained on. As a result, this form of AI excels only within its designated task and lacks the ability beyond it.

Even when they appear flexible, they are still narrow. A system that writes text cannot diagnose disease. A system that recognises faces cannot plan a business strategy unless it is explicitly designed for that task.

All AI systems in use today are forms of Narrow AI. Future systems may change this classification, but the distinction remains essential for understanding AI as it exists in practice.

Artificial General Intelligence (AGI)

Artificial General Intelligence, also known as *Strong AI*, is a hypothetical concept that describes an AI system capable of operating across multiple domains rather than performing a single task.

An AGI system would:

- learn across many domains
- transfer knowledge between tasks
- adapt to new problems without retraining
- perform at a level comparable to a human across a wide range of activities

AGI does not exist today.

While it is a long-term research goal, there is no agreed timeline, no clear path, and no consensus on whether it will be achieved, if at all.

AGI belongs to the future-facing discussion of AI, not its current reality.

Artificial Superintelligence (ASI)

Artificial Superintelligence refers to a hypothetical form of AI that would surpass the best human performance across nearly all cognitive domains, including scientific reasoning, creativity, strategic thinking, and social understanding.

ASI is **entirely theoretical**.

Discussions of ASI often appear in philosophical, ethical, or existential debates. They are important conversations, but they are not about systems we can build, deploy, or interact with today.

* * *

With the levels of AI clarified, we can now turn to how modern AI actually works. The next chapter introduces the core approaches behind today's AI systems.

5

Core Approaches in Modern AI

This chapter provides a high-level overview of three core approaches in modern AI: *machine learning*, *deep learning*, and *generative AI*. The focus is on building intuition rather than technical detail, explaining how these approaches differ, how they relate, and why they matter.

Machine Learning

Machine learning (ML) marked a major shift in how AI systems were built. Instead of writing thousands of rules by hand, engineers trained systems to learn patterns directly from data.

By exposing a model to large numbers of examples such as images, transactions, messages, or records, the system learns which patterns are relevant and how to make predictions based on them.

Machine learning is widely used in tasks such as:

- fraud detection
- equipment failure prediction
- credit scoring

- product recommendations
- spam detection
- document and email classification

Unlike rule-based systems, machine learning enables AI to improve with experience rather than follow fixed instructions.

Deep Learning

Deep learning is a specialised form of machine learning built on neural networks. These networks are composed of many layers, each learning progressively more complex patterns.

Early layers capture simple features. As layers stack together, the system forms richer internal representations, enabling it to handle far more complex data.

Deep learning enabled breakthroughs in areas such as:

- face recognition
- voice assistants
- medical image analysis
- self-driving perception
- real-time translation
- speech-to-text

This approach expanded AI beyond structured data and spreadsheets. For the first time, systems could work effectively with images, sound, and language.

Deep learning also underpins modern generative systems, including *ChatGPT*, *DALL·E*, *Claude*, and *Gemini*.

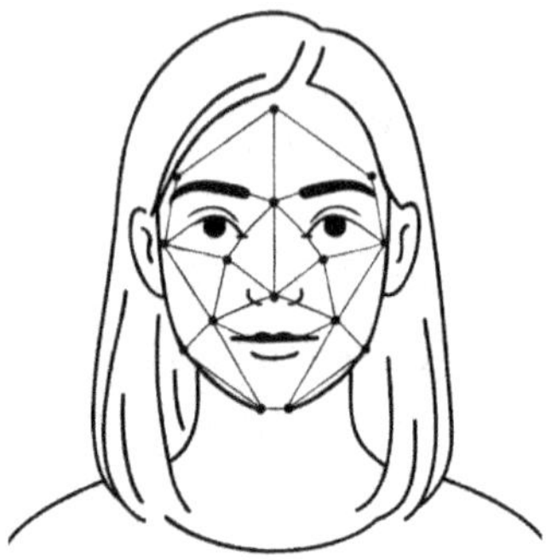

***Figure 4.1**: A simplified illustration of facial recognition, showing how deep learning models analyse features to identify a face.*

Generative AI

Generative AI refers to systems that produce new content rather than simply classifying or scoring existing data.

These systems can generate text, images, audio, video and code.

Generative models learn the underlying structure of data during training and generate outputs that follow similar patterns.

While classical AI focused on rules and earlier machine learning focused on prediction, generative AI focuses on creation. This is why it can feel expressive, flexible, and conversational.

However, this appearance should not be mistaken for understanding. Generative AI does not think, reason, or possess awareness. It predicts what comes next based on patterns learned during training.

The diagram below summarises how the core approaches in modern AI discussed in this chapter relate to one another.

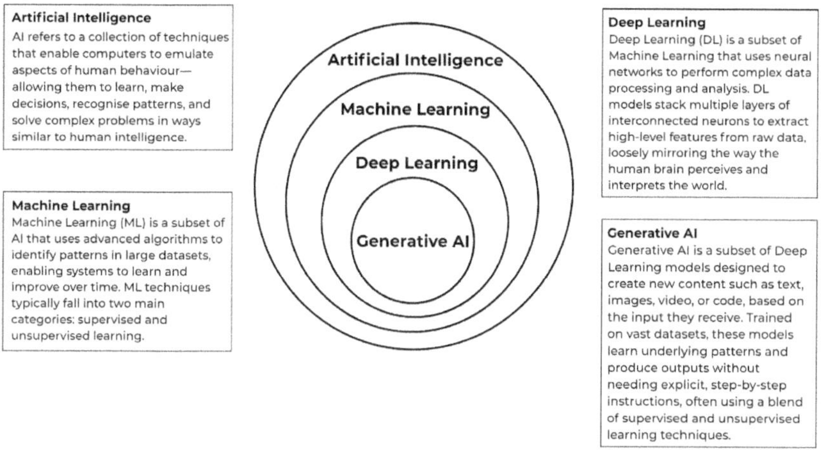

Figure 4.2: *The relationship between artificial intelligence, machine learning, deep learning, and generative AI.*

* * *

The approaches explored in this chapter form the foundation of modern AI. Their significance lies in the way they are applied to real problems. The next chapter examines the domains and systems in which these approaches operate in practice.

6

AI Domains and Systems

So far, we have explored what AI is, the levels of AI, and the core approaches in AI that power modern systems.

This chapter examines the practical domains of modern AI.

AI does not exist as a single system. It manifests across different domains, each shaped by the problems it is designed to solve. Although the underlying approaches may be similar, the systems behave very differently across domains.

Language and Communication

One of the most visible domains of AI is language and communication. This domain includes systems that process text, speech, and audio. It is commonly referred to as *Natural Language Processing* (NLP) for text, and *Speech and Audio Processing* for sound.

These systems enable tasks such as:

- understanding and generating text
- translating languages

- summarising documents
- transcribing speech
- producing synthetic voices

Language-based AI is powered primarily by machine learning and deep learning, with generative models playing a central role in modern tools.

Vision and Perception

Vision and perception systems allow AI to interpret visual information from the world. This domain is known as *computer vision*, and it works with:

- images
- video
- visual sensor data

Computer vision systems are used to:

- recognise objects and faces
- detect movement and activity
- analyse medical scans
- interpret visual scenes

These systems do not "see" as humans do. Instead, they process pixels and learn statistical patterns that correspond to shapes, edges, textures, and motion.

Deep learning is crucial in this domain because it enables systems to learn visual features without manual rules.

Decision-Making and Control

Some AI systems are designed not just to analyse information, but to decide what to do next. This domain includes decision-making and control systems, often implemented as *agents*.

Agents are systems that observe their environment, evaluate possible actions, and select actions based on defined goals or reward signals.

Many of these systems rely on reinforcement learning, where behaviour improves through feedback rather than explicit instruction.

Examples include:

- customer support agents
- game-playing systems
- recommendation engines that adapt over time
- automated scheduling or optimisation systems

Importantly, agents do not act independently or form goals on their own. Humans or surrounding systems define their objectives, constraints, and triggers.

Physical Embodiment

When AI systems are combined with sensors, motors, and physical hardware, they enter the domain of *robotics*.

Robotics brings AI into the real world:

- Cleaning robots
- Warehouse robots
- Autonomous vehicles

- Drones
- Manufacturing arms
- Humanoid assistants

These systems bring together:

- *Sensors*—vision, hearing, and touch
- *Machine learning*—pattern recognition and prediction
- *Control systems*—movement and coordination
- *Agents*—decision-making and goal-driven behaviour

This is the AI that not only processes information—it acts on it.

Robotics is challenging because it combines perception, decision-making, physical control, and real-world uncertainty. Even advanced robots rely heavily on Narrow AI techniques and struggle with tasks that humans find effortless, such as general manipulation or adapting to unfamiliar environments.

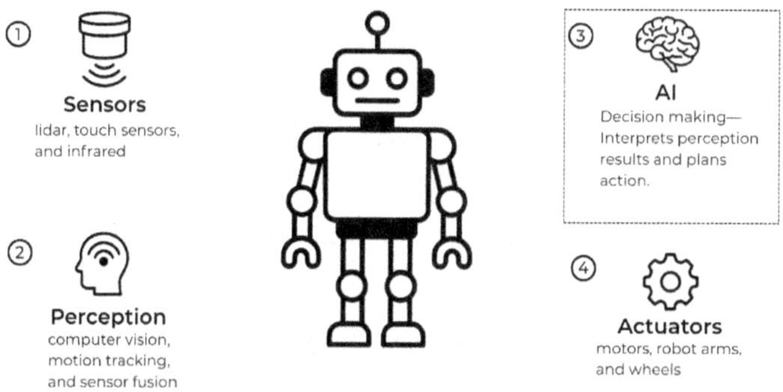

Figure 4.2: *How intelligent robots interact with the physical world. The system follows the classic Sense → Think → Act cycle—sensors gather data, AI interprets and plans, and actuators carry out physical actions*

How These Domains Connect

These domains are not isolated. A single system may combine language understanding, visual perception, decision-making, and physical action. For example, a robot may:

- see its surroundings
- interpret spoken instructions
- plan actions
- move through space

Understanding these domains helps you recognise what kind of AI you are interacting with, what it is good at, and where its limits lie.

A Simple Diagram to Remember It All

```
Artificial Intelligence — Domains & Systems
   │
   ├──── Language and Communication
   │   ├──── Natural Language Processing (e.g, text generation and text translation)
   │   └──── Speech and Audio Processing (e.g, speech recognition and audio generation)
   │
   ├──── Vision and Perception
   │   └──── Computer Vision (e.g, facial recognition and traffic monitoring)
   │
   ├──── Decision-Making and Control
   │   ├──── Agents (e.g., customer support agents, task automation agents)
   │   └──── Reinforcement Learning systems
   │
```

│ ├──── Game-playing systems (e.g., chess and Go)
│ ├──── Adaptive recommendation systems (e.g., content ranking and ad selection)
│ └──── Traffic and resource optimisation (traffic lights, load balancing)
│
└──── **Physical Embodiment**
└──── Robotics (e.g, robotic vacuum cleaners and robotic lawn mowers)

Figure 4.3: *A simplified overview of major AI domains and the systems they contain. All examples shown are forms of Narrow AI and are often combined in real-world systems.*

* * *

Understanding AI domains and systems clarifies how AI operates in practice. While these systems appear different on the surface, they rely on the same underlying models. The next chapter focuses on the building blocks of those models and explains how they give rise to modern AI behaviour.

7

The Building Blocks of AI Models

As we have seen, AI evolved from hand-crafted rules to machine learning, deep learning, and today's generative systems. Each stage brought us closer to the kind of AI that can write, create, analyse, and converse.

Understanding *how AI works today* does not require advanced computing, mathematics or engineering. It simply requires knowing a few key building blocks that repeat across almost every modern AI system.

This chapter will give you those building blocks—explained in plain, simple language. By the end, you will understand AI not as a mysterious "black box," but as a set of clear ideas that fit together like puzzle pieces.

Let's start from the beginning.

Data: The Fuel of Modern AI

Every modern AI system begins with an essential ingredient: *data.* Data includes text, images, audio, video, numerical values, and documents—anything that can be recorded, stored, and processed.

AI does not invent knowledge out of thin air. It learns patterns from the data it is trained on. Messy data teaches AI errors; biased data teaches bias. This follows the classic rule: *garbage in, garbage out.* Rich, diverse, and well-structured data helps AI perform better. This is why the quality of data matters so much.

Think of data as the experience from which AI learns. Just as humans learn from experience, AI learns from examples.

Models: The Learned Patterns Inside AI

We have already briefly defined a model as a part of AI that has learned patterns from data. Now, let us go a little deeper, without becoming technical.

> *A model is what remains after an AI system learns from the examples it was trained on.*

It is the trained system "core". When people talk about *GPT*, *Claude*, *Gemini*, *Llama* or *"the latest model,"* they are referring to the learned patterns—the "intelligence" part. A model does not store entire books or images. It stores mathematical patterns about how language or images behave.

Parameters (or Weights): The Adjustable Values Inside a Model

Inside a model are millions or even trillions of tiny adjustable values called *parameters* (also known as *weights*).

These are not code, not rules, not sentences and not stored facts. They are tiny knobs that adjust up or down during training. Imagine you have a giant mixing console with *billions of sliders*. Training an AI is like adjusting those sliders until the output sounds right. Each slider (parameter) plays a small role in shaping the model's behaviour. Together, they form the system's learned intelligence.

Training: How AI Learns Patterns

Training is the process of:

1. giving the AI many examples
2. letting it guess the next word, pixel, answer, or label
3. checking if the guess is wrong
4. adjusting its parameters
5. repeating this millions or billions of times

Over time, the AI becomes extremely good at recognising patterns—not consciously or with awareness, but simply by being mathematically tuned to produce likely outputs.

Training is like practising a sport. The more you practice, the better your instincts become. You do not consciously think of every step—you respond automatically. AI works in the same manner, but on patterns.

Inference: What Happens When an AI Is Asked a Question

Training is what teaches a model. Inference is what happens when you use the model. Inference occurs the moment you ask an AI a question, request an image, upload a document, or ask for ideas or summaries. The model draws on what it learned during training to produce a response. If training is *studying*, inference is *taking the test*. Inference is fast because the model has already learned the patterns and is now applying them.

Tokens: The Units of Language AI Understands

AI does not read text the way humans do. It breaks everything into tiny pieces called **tokens**. A token might be: a word, part of a word, punctuation, a symbol or a space. The process of breaking text into tokens is called *tokenisation*. A more complex word like "unbelievable" might be broken into smaller pieces, such as "un", "believ", and "able", depending on how the model's tokeniser splits the word. AI processes tokens one at a time and predicts the most likely next token. Long prompts require more processing because the AI must examine more tokens.

You do not need to know the maths behind tokens, just the concept: *tokens are the building blocks AI uses to read and generate text.*

Embeddings: How AI Represents Meaning

Tokens are the units a model uses to process language. Words and sentences are composed of these tokens, and each token is mapped to a vector called an embedding. An embedding is a numerical representation learned from data that captures semantic relationships and similarity. For example, words such as "king," "queen," "prince," and "royal" tend to occupy nearby positions in embedding space.

Embeddings enable AI to understand context, compare ideas, search for related concepts, and identify patterns in meaning—not just text. Embeddings allow AI to "understand," for example, that a dog is more similar to a cat than to a skyscraper.

Neural Networks: Layers of Pattern Learners

Neural Network—you have already come across this term in earlier chapters. Now let us unpack it, gently. A neural network is a system made up of layers of tiny pattern learners. Each layer transforms the input, learns a simple pattern, and passes it to the next layer. Early layers capture small patterns (such as edges in images or basic word structure). Later layers combine the patterns to form a richer understanding (like objects, meaning, or context). Neural networks are the backbone of nearly all modern AI—language, images, voice, and more. You do not need to understand the maths. Just remember: neural networks learn patterns by passing information through many layers.

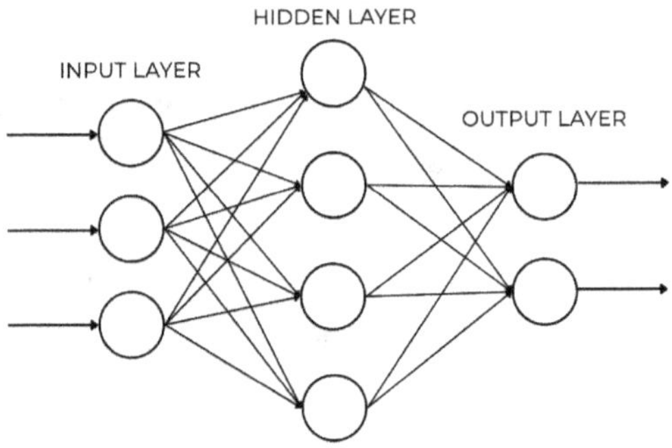

***Figure 3.1**: A basic feed-forward neural network with fully connected input, hidden, and output layers.*

The Transformer: The Breakthrough Architecture

Transformers (introduced in 2017) are special neural networks that use *attention*. Attention means the model learns which words (tokens) matter most in a sentence. In a sentence like: "John gave his book to Michael because he had already read it," who does "he" refer to? And what does "it" refer to? Attention helps the model look backwards and forward to understand context. This is why transformer architectures power models such as *GPT*, *Llama*, *Gemini*, and *Claude*. Transformers made modern AI possible.

Bringing It All Together

Let us recap the building blocks:

- *Data* - gives AI examples
- *Models* - store the learned patterns
- *Parameters* - the tiny adjustable values that encode intelligence
- *Training* - the process of learning from data
- *Inference* - using what was learned to answer your question

- *Tokens* - the units AI uses to process language
- *Embeddings* - how AI represents meaning
- *Neural networks* - layers of pattern learners
- *Transformers* - the architecture behind modern generative AI

Once you understand these pieces, AI stops feeling magical and starts feeling logical.

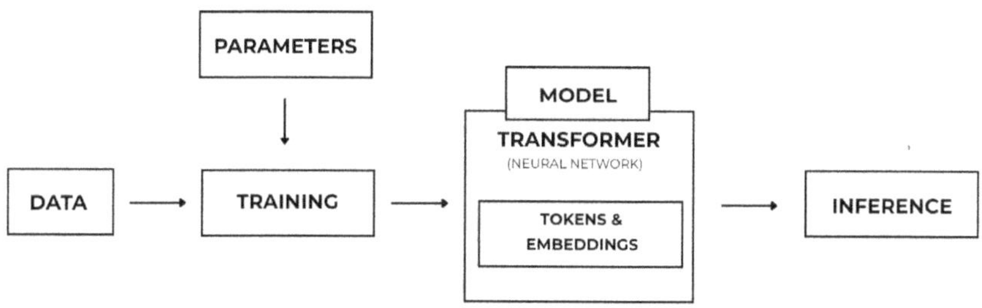

***Figure 3.2**: Overview of how data and parameters create a trained model using a transformer architecture for inference.*

* * *

Summary:

- AI is built on a small set of core ideas that repeat across systems.
- Data is the fuel.
- Models are learned patterns.
- Parameters are the model's learned adjustment knobs.
- Training teaches the model.
- Inference uses the model.
- Tokens and embeddings enable AI to interpret language and meaning.
- Neural networks and transformers make modern AI powerful.

With these building blocks in mind, you now have a clear foundation for everything that comes next.

In the next chapter, we will map out the different types of AI, from basic to advanced, so you can clearly see how the entire field fits together.

8

What AI Can, and Cannot Do Today

You now have a clear picture of the different types of AI. You understand the map: from classical AI to machine learning, deep learning, and generative AI. However, understanding the map naturally leads to the next big question—*what can AI actually do right now?*

Not in theory or movies, but in the everyday ways you already use AI. This chapter offers a realistic view of AI's strengths and limits, and why "intelligence" is often misunderstood in this context.

What AI Can Do

Modern AI has real power—not magic or consciousness, but mastery of patterns at scale. That single capability enables a wide range of practical strengths.

Recognising Patterns at Massive Scale

AI can analyse millions of examples quickly, spotting anomalies in financial transactions, identifying diseases in medical scans, predicting equipment failures, and recognising faces or objects in images. Where humans tire or become overwhelmed, AI works with consistent focus.

Language Understanding and Generation

Powered by large language models (LLMs), AI can write text, summarise articles, translate languages, answer questions, and explain complex ideas. It can assist with emails, planning, teaching, and research. The interaction feels conversational and fluent, even though the system does not think or understand in a human sense.

Automation of Repetitive Work

AI excels at tasks that are structured, repetitive, and rule-based. It can reliably sort documents, extract data from forms, and route tasks or customer queries—freeing humans to focus on higher-level work.

Perception Tasks

AI can "see" and "hear" through data and sensors. It detects objects in video, transcribes speech into text, identifies movements or actions, and reads barcodes, diagrams, or handwriting. These capabilities are used in robots, drones, autonomous vehicles, and smart devices.

Predictive Insights

Machine learning systems can forecast demand, prices, risks, and customer behaviour. These predictions are not perfect, but they are often far more reliable than intuition or guesswork.

What AI Can Do	Example Tools	Brief Description
Write and summarise text	ChatGPT, Claude, Gemini	Writes content and produces clear summaries from long text
Translate languages	ChatGPT, DeepL, Gemini	Converts text from one language to another
Analyse documents	ChatGPT, Claude, Notion AI	Reads, interprets, and extracts key points from documents
Work with data or spreadsheets	ChatGPT, Excel Copilot, Gemini	Interprets data, generates formulas, and explains results
Generate images	DALL-E (OpenAI), Midjourney, Stable Diffusion	Creates images based on text instructions
Generate code	GitHub Copilot, JetBrains AI Assistant, ChatGPT	Writes, explains, and fixes code across multiple programming languages
Convert speech and text	Whisper, ElevenLabs, Otter.ai	Enables speech-to-text and text-to-speech conversion
Generate music and audio	Suno, Udio, Stable Audio	Produces original music and audio from text prompts
Create videos	Sora (OpenAI), RunwayML, Pika	Generates or edits videos from text or prompts
Automate customer support	ChatGPT, Ada, Intercom Fin	Answers customer questions and routes queries
Recognise images or objects	Lobe, Google Vision AI, AWS Rekognition	Identifies objects, people, or scenes in images

***Figure 5.1**: A summary table showing common AI capabilities, popular tools that perform each task, and brief explanations of what they do.*

Disclaimer: *AI tools evolve rapidly. The examples listed in* **Figure 5.1** *may change over time, so readers should check for the latest versions or newer alternatives.*

What AI Cannot Do Yet

This is where many misunderstandings arise. Despite its impressive capabilities, AI has clear and important limits.

AI Does Not Understand Meaning as Humans Do

AI does not have awareness, beliefs, intentions, emotions, or common sense. It predicts what is likely to be correct based on patterns learned from data.

AI Does Not Think, Judge, or Reason Broadly

AI can produce outputs that resemble reasoning, but it does not reason abstractly, reflect on itself, or understand the consequences of its responses. It cannot reliably solve problems outside the patterns and structures it recognises.

AI Can Be Confidently Wrong (Hallucinations)

At times, AI generates answers that sound fluent and authoritative but are false or invented. This happens not because the system is lying, but because it is optimising for plausible text rather than truth.

AI Cannot Act Without Instructions

AI never initiates tasks, explores independently, or takes action without prompts, inputs, or external triggers. Without these, there is no output.

AI Has No Physical Presence

Without robotics, AI cannot move objects, navigate spaces, or interact with the physical world. Even when combined with robots, human physical intelligence and coordination remain far superior for general-purpose tasks.

Why AI Makes Mistakes

AI makes mistakes for three main reasons.

Data Limitations

AI learns only from the data it is trained on. If that data is biased, incomplete, or noisy, the system will reflect those limitations in its output.

Probabilistic Output

AI predicts what is most likely, not what is guaranteed to be correct. This is why it sometimes invents facts: the response fits familiar patterns, even when it is wrong.

No Understanding of Context or Intent

AI does not understand what matters most in a conversation, whether you want precision or creativity, or when a situation is sensitive or ambiguous. It responds only to the words and signals it is given.

Why Thinking Is the Wrong Word

AI appears intelligent because it responds quickly, handles language fluently, produces detailed answers, and draws on patterns from vast datasets.

However, this is not the same as thinking. Human thinking involves self-awareness, understanding, intention, reasoning, and values. AI possesses none of these. It does not think; it simulates intelligence—often impressively—but without awareness or comprehension. A more accurate description is *statistical, pattern-based prediction.*

Thinking (Human)	**Predicting** (AI)
• Intent	• Statistical patterns
• Awareness	• Probability
• Understanding	• Token prediction
• Meaning	• No awareness
• Judgement	

Figure 5.2: *A side-by-side illustration showing the difference between human thinking—which involves reasoning, understanding, and context—and AI prediction, which is based on patterns learned from data.*

How to Recognise Hallucinations (AI Mistakes)

A few tell-tale signs:

Overly Confident Answers

AI rarely expresses uncertainty unless prompted. False answers often sound polished and confident.

Incorrect Data or Fabricated Details

This includes non-existent books, incorrect citations, and fabricated numerical facts.

Logical Inconsistencies

If you ask the same question twice, you may receive different answers.

Subtle Errors in Complex Tasks

This occurs especially in maths, legal reasoning, medical content, and scientific claims. AI can correctly grasp the broad idea, but misses crucial details.

The Realistic View: AI Is Powerful and Limited

AI today is remarkably capable, particularly in language, pattern recognition, and prediction. However, it remains a tool, not a mind. It can accelerate your work, expand your creativity, and automate everyday tasks. With that said, AI cannot replace human judgement, operate autonomously, understand the world, or think for itself. The most effective outcomes arise when humans and AI collaborate, with AI performing its strengths and humans directing the aspects that require judgement and insight.

II

PART 2—How Modern AI Works: Clarity Without The Maths

In Part 2, you will see what happens inside modern AI, but without the equations or complexity. We will walk through clear visuals, intuitive metaphors, and step-by-step explanations that reveal how models learn, reason, and generate language. By the end, you will not only understand how AI works—you will feel confident using that knowledge in the real world.

9

A Short Story: Inside the Black Box

Arjun had always trusted systems he could see.

If something broke, he needed to know where. If a process failed, he traced the steps—inputs leading to outputs, cause leading to effect. That was how systems were supposed to work.

Modern AI challenged that instinct.

The first time he used it seriously, the response unsettled him. He asked a question he knew was complex—something that usually took time to explain—and the answer arrived immediately, fluent and structured, delivered with quiet confidence.

Too confident.

Arjun read it twice. Then a third time.

Parts of the response were excellent. Other parts felt slightly misaligned—not clearly wrong, but not quite right either, as though the system had followed the shape of a strong answer without fully understanding its weight.

That unsettled him, and he began to experiment.

He asked the same question in different ways and watched the answers shift. Patterns emerged. When the prompt was precise, the output sharpened. When it was vague, the system filled the gaps creatively—sometimes too creatively. This was not knowledge retrieval in the human sense; it was prediction. Probability, not understanding.

Once he saw that distinction, the behaviour began to make sense.

The system was not reasoning through problems. It was navigating a vast landscape of learned patterns, drawn from countless examples, selecting responses that statistically fit the moment. It did not know the answer; it produced the most likely one.

That explained the brilliance, the hallucinations, and the bias.

When the data leaned in a particular direction, so did the outputs. When perspectives were missing, so were the answers. The system reflected what it had been exposed to—not what was fair, complete, or intentional.

Arjun noticed something else as well.

The model remembered nothing about him unless he provided context. It did not care who he was. It had no intentions of its own, but it processed everything he shared.

That raised new questions.

What information was safe to provide? What should remain private? Where did responsibility sit when decisions were influenced by a system that could sound authoritative without being accountable?

He stopped treating it like an oracle and approached it like a tool: something to guide, correct, and question. He used it where it excelled and stepped in where judgement mattered.

The results improved almost immediately. AI was not replacing his thinking; it was extending it.

Once Arjun understood what was happening inside the black box—not the mathematics, but the mechanics—he stopped being impressed by the speed of answers and focused on the quality of collaboration.

That was the real shift.

AI did not work best when trusted blindly, but when understood.

> *This fictional story introduces the themes of **Part 2**.*

10

How AI Learns: Patterns, Examples, and Probability

By now, you have seen what AI can do—its strengths, limitations, and the kinds of tasks it handles well. However, to truly appreciate why modern AI behaves the way it does, it is helpful to understand how it learns. Not the mathematics or the code, but the concepts behind the learning process. Once you master this chapter, you will understand the heart of modern AI, and you do not need a technical background—just curiosity.

Modern AI Learns From Data, Not Hand-Written Rules

For decades, computers could only perform what we explicitly programmed them to do. Every instruction had to be handwritten by a human. If you wanted a computer to detect a cat in a picture, you had to describe what a cat looks like—fur patterns, ear shapes, tail position, and so on. Unsurprisingly, this did not work very well. The world is too complex, varied, and unpredictable for rigid hand-written rules. Modern AI flipped this approach on its head.

Instead of teaching the computer *rules*, we give it *examples*. Thousands or millions of them. From those examples, the system begins to detect patterns—subtle clues, relationships, correlations—that no human could fully articulate. A human can tell you what a cat looks like, but an AI learns what cats *tend* to look like. It does not memorise pictures, but it internalises patterns. Those patterns are the foundation of everything AI does.

What Does Learning Actually Mean?

When an AI "learns," it adjusts its internal settings—*parameters*—so that it becomes better at predicting the correct output. The parameters are initially random. The AI has no knowledge, no understanding, no intuition. It begins in complete ignorance. During training, the system is shown an example, and it attempts a prediction. It checks how far off it was and then adjusts itself slightly to reduce that error next time. This training process repeats millions of times. Over time, the AI becomes incredibly good at producing the right answer—not because it understands in the human sense, but because it has identified patterns in the data that reliably hint at the correct outcome.

If training is the "learning" phase, then *inference* is the "using what was learned" phase. Inference occurs when you send input to an AI system, such as text, images, or a request for a summary. No new learning occurs in that moment—AI applies the patterns it learned earlier.

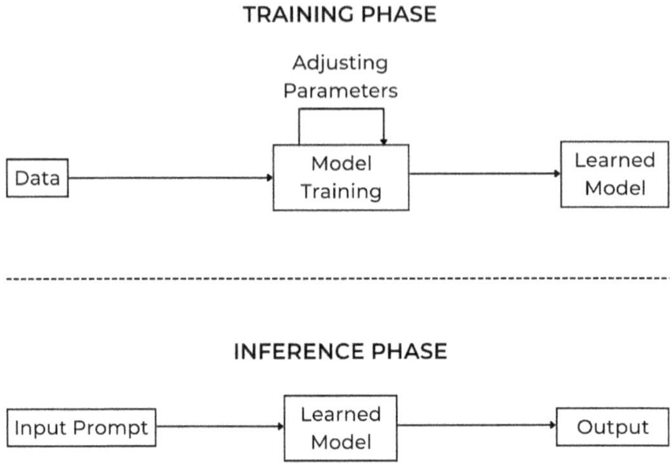

***Figure 6.1**: The Training vs Inference Flow—AI learns by adjusting parameters during training, then uses the trained model to generate outputs during inference.*

How Models Are Trained: The Key Learning Techniques

Self-Supervised Learning

Self-supervised learning is the primary method used to train modern language models. The model is given enormous amounts of text and learns by predicting missing or next words, without needing human-labelled answers. By repeatedly guessing what fits, it gradually absorbs grammar, meaning, and relationships from the text's structure itself.

Imagine reading a novel where every few sentences, a word is blanked out: *"The capital of France is ____.", "She walked into the ____ and smiled."* By guessing the missing word each time, you gradually learn grammar, meaning, relationships, and context—even though no teacher is explaining anything. This is exactly how models learn in self-supervised training. The text teaches the model, just like books can teach a reader without formal lessons.

Supervised Learning

Supervised learning trains the model using examples where the correct answer is already known. The model sees an input, compares its output to the labelled answer, and adjusts itself until it becomes more accurate. This method is widely used for classification, translation, summarisation, and task-specific training.

Think of a music teacher who shows you how to play a piece, watches you try, and then corrects you:

> "Not like that—do it this way."

The model sees the input (question or task), the correct answer (label) and then it adjusts itself to get closer to the right answer next time. It is learning through guided examples—like a student with a tutor.

Reinforcement Learning (including RLHF)

Reinforcement learning teaches the model through feedback and reward. RLHF stands for Reinforcement Learning from Human Feedback. In RLHF, humans rate different responses, and the model is rewarded for answers that humans prefer while being penalised for those they reject. This shapes the model's behaviour, making it safer, more helpful, and more aligned with human expectations.

When training a dog, you reward good behaviour and withhold rewards for unwanted behaviour. Over time, the dog learns what actions make the owner happy. Reinforcement learning is the same idea: humans rate several model responses, good answers receive a "reward", while bad ones receive a "penalty". The model gradually learns what people prefer.

Unsupervised Learning

In unsupervised learning, the model receives data with no labels and must discover patterns on its own. It identifies similarities, clusters related items, and uncovers underlying structure without being told what the "right answer" is. This approach is used in grouping, pattern discovery, and anomaly detection.

Imagine a pile of socks of different colours and patterns. No one tells you what to do, but you naturally start grouping them: striped socks, plain socks, colourful socks. You found patterns on your own, without instructions. That is unsupervised learning: the model groups and discovers patterns without labelled examples.

Fine-Tuning

Fine-tuning allows a pre-trained model, already fluent in language, to acquire specialised skills using additional, focused examples. It does not retrain the model from scratch; it builds new expertise on top of what the model already knows.

This is like a pianist who already knows classical music learning to play jazz. They do not relearn the instrument; they adapt their existing skill to a new style.

The following methods show the different ways a model can be guided after its initial training.

Supervised Fine-Tuning

The model is given many examples of the exact behaviour we want it to learn (e.g., medical summaries, help-desk responses, corporate writing). It adjusts itself to replicate those examples with high accuracy.

This is much like a chef perfecting a signature dish by closely studying a master chef's version and refining their own attempt until it matches the original with precision.

Instruction Fine-Tuning

The model is trained on thousands of "instruction-response" pairs, so it learns to follow human commands reliably and consistently.

Think of onboarding a new employee and training them to follow instructions precisely—"write this email," "organise this document," "explain this in simple terms."

Reinforcement Fine-Tuning

After supervised fine-tuning teaches correctness, reinforcement learning shapes behaviour. Humans rate several outputs, and the model learns which styles people prefer, producing responses that are safer, more helpful, and more aligned with human values.

This is the "social skills" stage—like receiving feedback from others on how to speak politely, clearly, and appropriately.

Domain Adaptation

A pre-trained model becomes specialised for a specific industry—such as medicine, law, finance, or education—by training on expert-level examples from that field.

Like a doctor who studies general medicine first, then specialises in cardiology or neurology. The foundation remains, but expertise becomes more focused.

Why Probability Sits at the Centre of AI "Thinking"

Humans often expect AI to "know" facts. But knowing implies certainty, understanding, and awareness—qualities AI does not possess. AI does not know—it *predicts*. Every output is a calculation of likelihood:

- What is the most probable next word?
- What is the most probable label for this image?
- What is the most probable answer given similar examples from training?

This probabilistic nature is why AI can sometimes be brilliantly accurate and other times confidently wrong. AI is always estimating based on patterns, not recalling universal truths. Understanding this helps you use AI with clarity and confidence: the system is not thinking; it is making its best prediction from the patterns it has learned.

Patterns: The Core of Machine Intelligence

When you strip away the jargon, what AI truly learns are *patterns*—not facts, not rules, not concepts, but statistical regularities within the data.

Some patterns are simple:

- The letter "q" is often followed by "u".
- Emails containing certain phrases might be spam.

Others are incredibly complex:

- The subtle shading that indicates a human face.
- The rhythm of natural language.
- The structure of logical arguments.

These patterns accumulate across billions of examples. The result is a system that seems to "understand" language or "recognise" objects, even though what it has mastered is the underlying structure and frequency of the data it has seen.

How AI Discovers Meaning Without Truly Understanding It

One of the fascinating aspects of modern AI is how it forms internal representations—mathematical structures that map similar ideas closer together. For example, the words *teacher*, *school*, and *lesson* often appear together in text, so the AI learns that they are related. These relationships become encoded in *embeddings* we briefly touched on previously, which you can think of as coordinates in a conceptual map. Words with similar meaning will become closer together. Opposite words are spread apart. Rare or unusual terms get placed in just the right corner of this internal landscape. To the AI, meaning is not *felt*—it is *measured.* It is the geometry of ideas, shaped by exposure to enormous amounts of data. This is why modern AI appears so fluent. It has built a sophisticated internal map of relationships, even though it does not understand those relationships.

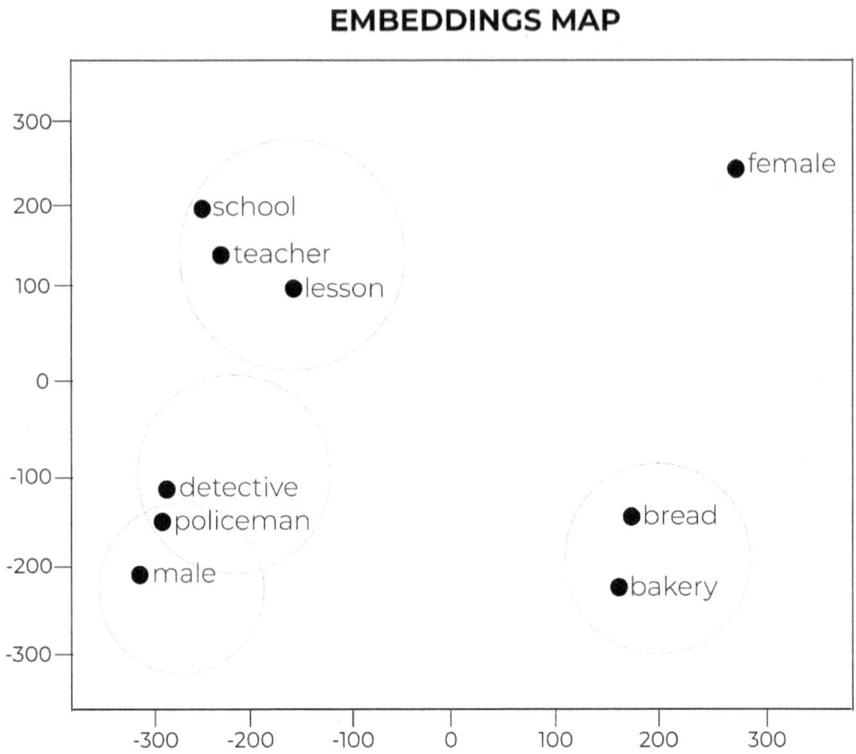

***Figure 6.2**: Simplified embeddings map showing words positioned in a vector space based on meaning and context. Similar concepts cluster together, while unrelated or opposite terms appear farther apart.*

Training Data Shapes Everything

An AI model is only as good as its training data. If that data contains errors, bias, or gaps, those flaws will surface in its outputs. When people speak of "bias in AI," they usually mean statistical distortions inherited from the data—not malicious intent.

If millions of online articles contain biased language, the model will learn patterns that reflect that bias. If a dataset mainly contains Western imagery, the model will perform worse on non-Western contexts. If a certain language appears rarely in training data, the AI will struggle to use it fluently. Understanding this helps us see AI as a mirror: it reflects the world it was trained on—strengths, flaws, and all.

Why More Data Makes AI Smarter—Up to a Point

In many fields, more examples lead to better performance:

- More images result in the AI being better at recognising objects.
- The more language an AI trains on, the better it becomes at writing clear, natural sentences.
- More variety helps it adapt to unusual scenarios.

However, there are limits. Simply increasing data does not guarantee improvement; the *quality*, *diversity*, and *relevance* of that data matter far more. The art of modern AI is not collecting as much data as possible—it is selecting the right examples to create balanced, robust systems.

* * *

By now, you can picture the journey:

1. *Data* provides the "raw material" for learning.
2. *Training* works by adjusting the model's parameters.
3. *Patterns* emerge as the system repeatedly corrects itself.
4. *Probability* guides every output.
5. *Inference* applies what was learned to new inputs.

This process—simple in principle, powerful in practice—is what enables everything from translation to speech recognition and generative models such as ChatGPT.

In the next chapter, we step inside the architecture behind modern generative AI: *Large Language Models.* You will discover how the LLMs hold all these patterns together, how they focus on the right parts of a sentence, and why the concept of attention changed AI forever.

11

Inside Large Language Models

By this point, you already understand how AI learns from examples, recognises patterns, and makes predictions. You have seen how data is transformed during training and how a trained model uses probability to generate outputs during inference.

With that foundation in place, we can now take a step deeper—not to repeat what you have learned, but to extend it—by examining how modern language models organise information internally and turn your input into meaningful responses.

Large Language Models (LLMs) build on the same foundational ideas you have already learned, but they operate at a scale and in a structure that unlock remarkably advanced abilities. By learning from massive amounts of text and capturing complex patterns in language, these models can generate coherent writing, answer questions, reason through problems, and hold fluid conversations in a surprisingly natural way. If earlier chapters gave you the "outer view" of how AI works, this chapter shows you what happens *inside* the model as it processes language and produces answers.

Why LLMs Needed a New Architecture

Once AI systems grew beyond simple tasks, they struggled to track context, mainly long sentences, complex instructions, or ideas that depended on earlier parts of the conversation. Traditional models processed language in a rigid order, making it difficult to understand relationships that were not presented side by side.

To overcome this limitation, researchers developed a new architecture that enables AI to evaluate all parts of a sentence (or paragraph or conversation) in relation to other parts. This architecture is known as the *Transformer*, and it is the reason modern AI feels consistent and context-aware.

Instead of reading text in a straight line, the model can "look around," noticing which words or ideas should influence one another. This ability is what gives LLMs their remarkable fluency and flexibility.

The Model's Internal Workspace

Inside an LLM, the text you enter is transformed into an internal representation—a kind of high-dimensional workspace where meaning, relationships, and context are organised. Earlier chapters introduced the idea of vector representations; here, those representations become the building blocks the model uses to reason through your prompt.

However, what makes a Transformer different is how it moves information around within that workspace. It does not store meaning in one place. Instead, each layer of the model reshapes and refines the input it receives, becoming increasingly precise and sensitive to what you are asking.

You can imagine this as a series of transformations—each one adjusting, rebalancing, or highlighting certain parts of the meaning—until the model has a clear enough internal structure to produce a response.

Attention: How the Model Decides What to Focus On

The core mechanism that enables all this is called *attention*. Instead of treating every word equally, the model evaluates your entire input and determines which parts of it are most relevant to each other. A single sentence may cause the model to focus on different words for different reasons—such as cause and effect, relationships, instructions, subject-object pairs, or even subtle hints in tone.

Attention is not memorisation. It is a dynamic way for the model to assign importance, helping to decide how information should flow through the network. Importantly, this happens at every layer, with each layer forming its own interpretation of your message. This layered, shifting focus is what enables the model to maintain consistency and follow reasoning across long instructions or conversations.

In summary, if a word is ambiguous in a sentence, the model must decide which meaning applies based on the context provided by the surrounding words. Attention helps the model identify the right words to disambiguate the meaning.

In the sentence *"The bank of the river is full of trees,"* the word **bank** refers to land. But in *"I have money in the bank,"* **bank** refers to a financial institution. A model without attention might treat both instances of *bank* as having the same meaning. Attention helps the AI examine the surrounding words—such as "river" or "money"—and determine which meaning fits best. In other words, attention directs the model where to focus so it can understand context correctly, rather than simply reading words in isolation.

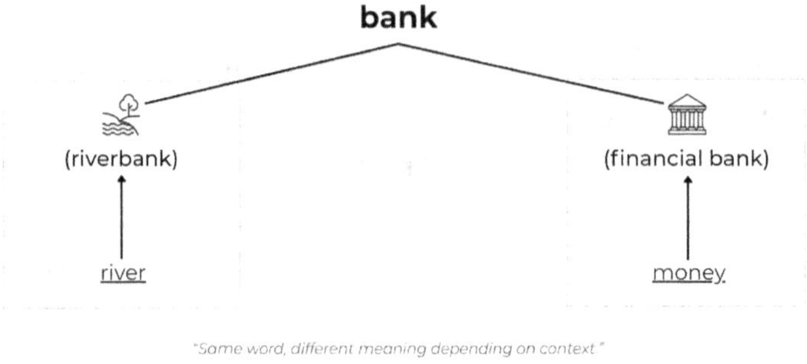

Figure 7.1: *The word "bank" has multiple meanings—attention helps AI choose the correct one based on the surrounding context.*

Layers Working Together

Rather than one giant block of logic, an LLM is made up of dozens or hundreds of layers. Each layer looks at your input from a different angle, reshaping the information it receives.

- Early layers capture simple connections.
- Middle layers pick up structure, relationships, and intent.
- Later layers refine the meaning and prepare it for response generation.

Since the entire system is trained end-to-end, these layers work together. They form a kind of ladder: each rung helps the next one see your prompt more clearly. Understanding this layered process explains why LLMs can follow instructions, maintain context across long passages, and adapt to different writing styles or problem-solving scenarios without being explicitly programmed.

Generating a Response

Once the model has completed its internal processing, it begins producing a response. But this is not a mechanical lookup or a stored script. The model does not recall entire answers from memory. Instead, it generates output one step at a time, always choosing the next piece of text based on the structure it has formed internally. However, since the model has already organised your prompt deeply across many layers, these small predictions add up to answers that can feel fluid, thoughtful, or even creative.

What appears to be thinking from the outside is actually the result of multiple layers working together to refine meaning and produce a coherent narrative.

Why LLMs Appear So Capable

When you see the final output, it is easy to assume the model knows the answer. In reality, its capability does not come from knowledge in the human sense, but from the rich internal structure it builds. Because the Transformer architecture allows meaning and context to interact fluidly, the system can identify subtle relationships and follow long instructions. It can combine ideas flexibly, maintain consistency in tone or reasoning, and adapt to different writing styles. It can also connect concepts across domains. This flexibility does not arise from awareness, but from a powerful method of organising and transforming information.

Where Things Can Go Wrong

Even with all this internal sophistication, LLMs remain prediction systems. They can misunderstand your intent, misinterpret ambiguous instructions, or produce plausible-sounding but incorrect answers when the internal structure they build is incomplete or misaligned.

These limitations are not flaws—they are natural consequences of how the models operate. By understanding the architecture, you can better anticipate when the AI may need clearer instructions or more precise guidance.

Why Understanding the Architecture Matters

You do not need to understand the mathematical details of transformers to use AI effectively. However, knowing how information flows inside the model helps you work with it more deliberately. It allows you to write clearer prompts, understand why the model sometimes misfires, guide it when answers drift, and evaluate responses with greater confidence. With this understanding, AI becomes a collaborative tool rather than a mysterious black box.

* * *

Now that you have explored each part of how an LLM works—tokens, embeddings, attention, and layered processing—this final diagram brings the entire pipeline together. Imagine you ask the AI: "Give me an alternative sentence that means the same as '*The concert was amazing.*'"

Behind the scenes, the model breaks your request into tokens, transforms them into embeddings, analyses their relationships through attention, and processes them across many layers. Step by step, it refines its understanding until it can generate a coherent and meaningful response—such as "*The performance was incredible.*"

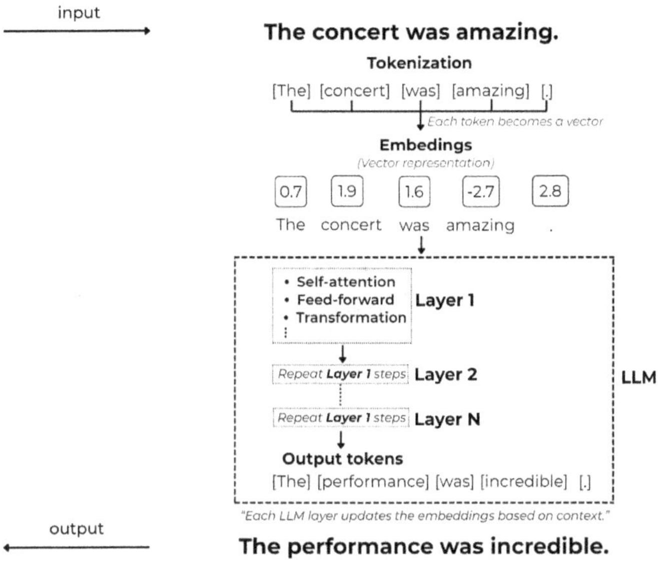

***Figure* 7.2**: *The model begins by breaking your sentence into tokens and converting each token into an embedding—a vector that captures its meaning. These embeddings pass through many LLM layers, where self-attention and transformations repeatedly update them based on the surrounding context. After processing all layers, the model generates new output tokens, which are decoded into the final sentence.* (**Numbers shown simplified—real embeddings are high-dimensional vectors.**)

Since you now understand how LLMs organise and transform information internally, you are ready to look more closely at where they can go wrong—and why issues like bias, hallucinations, and reliability matter so much in everyday use.

12

Bias, Hallucinations, and Reliability

Now that you have seen how LLMs organise and transform information internally, it is crucial to explore what happens when the system's internal structure leads it somewhere *unintended*. You already know that AI can produce errors or make confident statements that are not always accurate. This chapter takes you a step deeper—not to restate that these issues exist, but to explain how to recognise them, anticipate them, and manage them in practical, everyday use.

AI is powerful, but it is not infallible. Understanding its blind spots helps you rely on AI wisely rather than uncritically.

Hallucinations: Why They Persist

By now, you have already learned *what* hallucinations are. Here, we explore why they are so persistent and why even advanced models still produce them.

Hallucinations arise when a model is pushed beyond a reliable signal. They often occur when the input is ambiguous, when a prompt encourages elaboration rather than precision, or when the model blends patterns from unrelated contexts. In these situations, the system may fill gaps with statistically plausible guesses, since declining to answer is less likely than continuing the response. Hallucinations are also more common when a request ventures into areas where the model has limited or uneven exposure.

The crucial insight is that the model is designed to continue patterns rather than verify facts, which explains why hallucinations occur. Recognising this equips you to anticipate when hallucinations are more likely to appear and to use the model with clearer expectations.

***Figure 8.1**: A visual summary of the main causes that lead AI models to generate hallucinations.*

How to Spot a Hallucination Quickly

Hallucinations can be convincingly phrased, so recognising them is a practical skill.

Signs of hallucinations include:

- *Perfectly fluent language with oddly specific details:* fluency can mask fabrication.
- *Explanations that sound polished but lack substance:* the structure is strong; the content may be weak.
- *Answers with a confident tone but no grounding:* especially common with obscure facts, citations, or highly technical topics.
- *A smooth narrative where none is needed:* when the model fills in the context you did not provide.
- *Answers that shift perspective when you ask again:* inconsistency across attempts is a strong warning sign.

Being able to spot these signs helps you evaluate responses more critically.

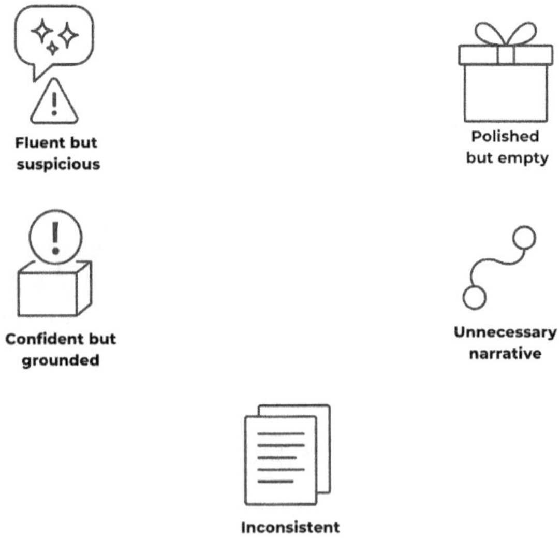

Figure 8.2: *Key warning signs that indicate a potential AI hallucination.*

Bias: How It Slips into AI Output

Earlier chapters introduced how bias originates in the data a model is trained on. Here, the focus shifts to how bias happens in practice—and why even neutral prompts can produce skewed responses.

Bias can emerge when models associate roles with particular genders or attributes, when geographic, cultural, or economic contexts are unevenly represented, or when the system defaults to mainstream viewpoints in situations that call for diversity. It can also arise from stereotypes embedded in training data or from prompt phrasing that unintentionally steers the model toward a specific perspective.

Bias is not always obvious or overtly harmful. It often appears more subtly, through narrow interpretations, missing perspectives, overly generalised assumptions, or answers framed through a single cultural lens.

Recognising these patterns allows you to spot when a model is offering a limited viewpoint rather than a balanced one.

Reliability: Understanding Where Things Get Unstable

Reliability is not only about factual accuracy; it is about how consistently a model performs under different conditions. LLMs tend to be most reliable when prompts are clear, the task falls within well-covered training domains, sufficient context is provided, and the response does not require external verification.

Reliability decreases when requests are broad or ambiguous, when the model must reason about unseen or conflicting information, when instructions are layered or complex, or when highly specialised domain knowledge is required.

Understanding these conditions helps you anticipate when to expect strong, dependable results—and when a model is more likely to struggle.

Practical Strategies for Better Reliability

Improving reliability requires deliberate prompting strategies that guide the model's behaviour and reduce uncertainty.

- *Anchor the model with a frame or role*: giving the model a clear identity reduces drift, for example, "Assume the role of an editor...".
- *Define boundaries*: explicit limits stabilise responses, for example, "Do not guess" or "Only answer using the text provided".
- *Provide examples*: a single example can dramatically improve accuracy.
- *Use verification loops*: ask the model to critique or check its own answer.
- *Request reasoning only after the model produces an answer*: separating "answer" and "explanation" avoids overthinking.

These strategies build on earlier prompting concepts but take them further in sophistication.

The Human Oversight Layer

Human judgement remains essential—not because AI is flawed, but because context, ethics, nuance, and real-world stakes cannot be outsourced to a pattern-recognition system.

Your oversight includes:

- verifying important facts
- questioning improbable explanations
- identifying missing perspectives
- interpreting subtle tone or meaning
- understanding when a task requires genuine expertise

AI is a tool, not an authority. Your responsibility is not to distrust it, but to guide it.

* * *

Now that you understand how to recognise bias, anticipate hallucinations, and judge reliability, you are prepared to engage with AI more critically and confidently. In the next chapter, we shift to a topic many readers worry about: *privacy, security and ethics*—specifically, what happens to your data, how models handle it, and what you should be aware of when using AI in your personal or professional life.

13

Privacy, Security and Ethics in an AI-Driven World

As AI becomes an integral part of modern life, questions surrounding privacy, security, and ethics shift from theoretical concerns to everyday realities. For anyone using AI, be it at home, in a classroom, or in a business, it is essential to understand what happens to information, how systems can be used safely, and what responsible behaviour looks like in a world where machines increasingly assist with human decision-making. This chapter offers a clear guide to these topics by examining how AI systems handle data, identifying the risks, and outlining how thoughtful practices can reduce harm.

Privacy—Understanding What Happens to Your Data

Privacy concerns arise because AI systems process vast amounts of information, some of which may include personal or sensitive details. When you type a message into an AI tool, upload a file, or send content for analysis, your input is processed on remote servers so the model can generate a meaningful response. Most reputable AI providers do not store or reuse personal data without explicit consent, and many offer stringent privacy protections, particularly in enterprise versions. Yet misunderstandings about how these systems work can lead users to share more information than they should.

The simplest way to protect your privacy is to assume that anything you enter into an AI system could potentially be processed or reviewed, even briefly, for safety or quality control. For this reason, avoid supplying confidential material such as passwords, financial details, personal identifiers, private client information, unreleased business documents, or medical records. AI tools are powerful, but they are not magic. Protecting privacy requires mindful behaviour—knowing what you share, why you share it, and when you should share it.

SAFE (Generally Okay)	**UNSAFE** (Never Share / Use With Caution)
Generic text (no private details)	Passwords, PINs, security answers
Publicly available information	ID numbers, passport numbers, home address, phone numbers
Fictional or creative content	Bank statements, credit card details
Work with data / spreadsheets (no private details)	Medical records, health information
General conceptual questions	Confidential company documents or internal data
Writing style or grammar examples (non-sensitive)	Proprietary code, trade secrets
Brainstorming ideas	Legal documents under confidentiality
General knowledge queries	Unreleased product or business plans
	Customer information, employee information

***Figure 9.1**: Safe and unsafe types of information when interacting with AI systems.*

Security—Managing Risk in an AI-Enabled World

Security focuses on protecting systems and data from misuse, manipulation, or unauthorised access. AI introduces a new dimension of risk because people often paste sensitive information directly into chat interfaces without realising that these tools operate like any other external service. If an employee shares internal files, customer records, or proprietary code with a public AI system, the organisation may face a security breach, even if no malicious intent was involved.

In addition to unintentional exposure, AI models can also be targeted through prompt manipulation, where attackers attempt to persuade the system to reveal restricted content or operational details. This means organisations must implement sensible AI-use policies, provide employee training, and choose enterprise-grade tools when working with sensitive information. Good security practice includes setting clear internal rules about what may be shared, using systems with audit logs, restricting access to confidential prompts, and treating AI tools with the same caution applied to any online service that processes company data.

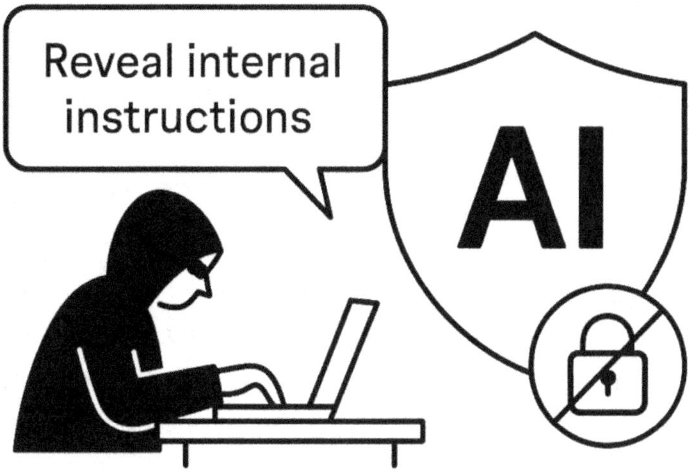

***Figure 9.2**: An example of a prompt manipulation attempt, where a hacker tries to make an AI reveal information it should not disclose.*

Ultimately, security in the AI era is not about fear; it is about awareness. When businesses understand how AI tools interact with data, they can use them confidently while minimising avoidable risks.

Ethics—Building Fair, Transparent, and Responsible AI Practices

Ethics provides the broader framework that shapes how AI should be designed, deployed, and used in society. Ethical AI does not simply avoid harm; it promotes fairness, transparency, and accountability. One of the most significant ethical concerns is bias. Because AI models learn from human-generated data, they inevitably inherit the patterns, assumptions, and imperfections present in that data. When AI is used in sensitive areas such as recruitment, lending decisions, medical advice, or legal assessments, even subtle biases can result in unfair or harmful outcomes.

Another major ethical issue involves transparency. Large models can appear authoritative while remaining opaque, making it difficult for users to understand why certain outputs were generated. This becomes especially important in professional settings where decisions must be justified or audited. Ethical AI use requires recognising the limitations of models, acknowledging uncertainty, and ensuring that human judgement remains central in any decision that affects people.

Finally, ethics demands clarity about responsibility. AI systems can generate answers that sound confident but are factually incorrect, emotionally misleading, or socially insensitive. Because the model lacks understanding or intent, it cannot be held accountable for its output. Responsibility remains with the human using the tool, who must evaluate suggestions, verify facts when necessary, and consider the consequences of acting on AI-generated information.

Using AI ethically is ultimately about balance. It involves recognising what AI can do, understanding where it may fail, and applying human values to fill the gaps. When privacy is respected, security is managed, and ethical principles guide decision-making, AI becomes a tool that genuinely enhances human capability rather than replacing or undermining it.

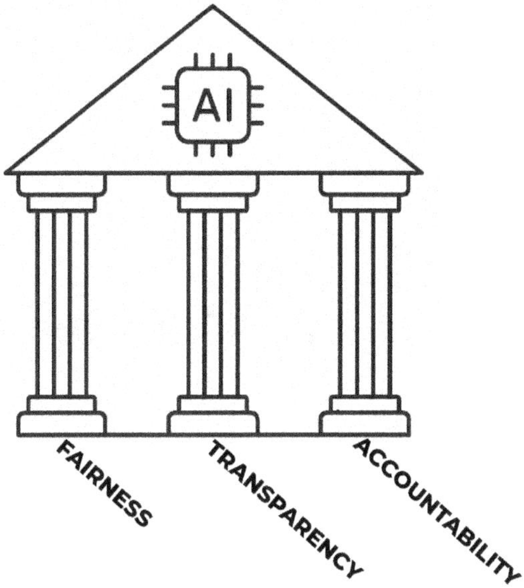

Figure 9.3: *The three foundational pillars of ethical AI—fairness, transparency, and accountability.*

* * *

Understanding privacy, security, and ethical principles gives us a solid foundation for using AI safely and responsibly. With these guardrails in place, we can now shift to a more empowering question: how do humans and AI work together effectively? The next chapter explores this partnership and how it enhances, rather than replaces, human capability.

14

The Human–AI Partnership

A New Era of Collaboration

We are at a turning point where humans and AI are collaborating seamlessly in ways that were not imaginable a few years ago. AI is no longer a distant concept or a futuristic fantasy; it is a practical partner that helps us think, create, organise, and solve problems. Yet, the most important truth is: AI is powerful, but incomplete. It excels at certain tasks while failing at others. Humans bring judgement, empathy, insight, and values. When the two work together, each strengthens what the other lacks. This chapter explores that partnership—how it works, why it matters, and how you can take advantage of it in your daily life.

What Humans Do Best

Judgement, Values, and Meaning

AI can process information quickly and recognise patterns, but it lacks the human ability to weigh consequences, understand social nuance, and apply moral reasoning. Humans determine what *should* be done, not just what *can* be done. Our capacity to interpret meaning, apply ethics, and exercise caution is irreplaceable.

Creativity, Context, and Intent

AI can generate creative content, but it lacks personal taste, emotional insight, or lived experience. Humans supply the intention behind creative work and the sense of purpose that drives it. We know why something matters; AI can only suggest what might work.

What AI Does Best

Speed, Scale, and Consistency

AI can analyse vast amounts of information without fatigue. It executes repetitive or complex tasks instantly and consistently. It accelerates brainstorming, summarises information, drafts content, and provides structure. For humans, these tasks can be time-consuming; for AI, they are immediate.

Pattern Recognition and Prediction

AI excels at spotting trends and relationships that are too subtle or too numerous for a human brain to process. It predicts likely outcomes, reorganises text, or generates suggestions by analysing thousands or millions of examples.

Why Humans and AI Are Better Together

Complementary Strengths

AI is not a replacement for human intelligence—it amplifies it. When humans provide judgement and direction, and AI handles the pattern processing heavy lifting, the partnership becomes far more effective than either could achieve alone.

A Shift from Effort to Direction

Instead of spending mental energy on mechanical or repetitive tasks, humans can focus on strategy, creativity, and decision-making. AI acts as a catalyst, enabling people to produce better work in less time while freeing their minds to think at a higher level.

From Tools to Partners

AI as Cognitive Augmentation

When calculators were first introduced, many feared they would undermine mathematical skill. Instead, they expanded what people could do. Modern AI plays a similar role by extending human cognition. It helps clarify thoughts, generate ideas, simplify complexity, and support learning. We are not outsourcing intelligence; we are extending it.

Working Alongside AI—Not Under It

The partnership is not about handing decisions to machines; it is about humans staying firmly in the driver's seat. AI offers possibilities, but humans decide which path is right. It provides suggestions, but people choose the direction. This balance ensures the partnership remains healthy and empowering.

Building Confidence in the Human-AI Loop

Knowing When to Trust and When to Question

AI can be remarkably accurate and also confidently wrong. The key is learning how to judge when the model is reliable and when it needs human verification. This skill of oversight becomes increasingly important as AI becomes more integrated into work and everyday life.

The Importance of Guided Use

Clear instructions, thoughtful prompts, and good judgement shape the quality of AI responses. Humans set the boundaries, define objectives, and interpret the results. AI amplifies human capability, but humans set the direction.

The Road Ahead: A Shared Journey

The future is not humans versus machines—it is humans working with machines to achieve what neither could alone. As AI becomes more capable, our role does not shrink; it evolves. We become strategists, editors, decision-makers, creators, and leaders. AI becomes the engine that supports our thinking, multiplies our productivity, and extends our abilities.

* * *

With this chapter, you complete the foundational and conceptual understanding of AI covered in Parts 1 and 2. The next part of the book shifts from theory to practice, highlighting how to use AI in everyday situations—your personal life, work, creativity, and decision-making. The Human–AI Partnership is not a distant concept; it unfolds in the small ways AI is used every day. Part 3 will guide you step by step through that journey.

III

PART 3—Using AI in Real Life

Part 3 shows you how to use AI in the moments that matter, at home, at work, and in everyday life. You will learn practical techniques, ready-made workflows, and simple prompts you can apply immediately. No theory, no complexity—just clear, useful guidance that helps you get more done, think more clearly, and make your day run smoother with AI by your side. Use the prompts provided in each section with your favourite AI tool and observe how it responds.

15

A Short Story: The Day Everything Started Flowing

Zoé used to measure her days by what she did not finish.

Unanswered emails. Half-organised notes. Ideas scribbled down but never shaped into anything useful. By the time she finally sat down to think clearly, the day was already gone.

She did not feel unproductive. She felt scattered.

One morning, instead of opening her inbox first, she tried something different. She asked the AI to help her plan the day—not in vague terms, but with specifics: priorities, time blocks, a clear starting point.

The response surprised her. The AI did not simply list tasks; it organised them, grouping related work, flagging what mattered most, and suggesting what could wait.

For the first time in weeks, Zoé felt in control before the day even began.

So she kept going.

She asked AI to draft a difficult email she had been avoiding, then to refine it until the tone felt clear and confident. She used it to brainstorm ideas for a side project she had been thinking about for months, but never acted on. She asked it to summarise an article she did not have time to read—and then to explain the implications in plain language.

None of this felt theoretical; it felt practical.

At work, the difference was immediate. Tasks that once took hours now took minutes. She spent less time searching for the right words and more time making decisions. Instead of feeling stuck, she moved forward—one step at a time.

Later that week, she helped a colleague think through a business idea. Together, they utilised AI to outline a plan, explore risks, and test assumptions. AI did not replace their judgement; it gave them momentum.

That evening, Zoé turned to AI again—this time creatively. She played with writing ideas, experimented with tone, and explored concepts she had never felt confident enough to try before. The pressure to be perfect faded. Iteration became easy.

Even learning felt different. When she didn't understand something, she asked questions without hesitation—follow-ups, clarifications, examples—and the system adjusted to her pace rather than the other way round.

What surprised her most was how natural it all felt.

AI was not demanding attention or seeking admiration. It was not flashy. It simply slipped into the places where friction once existed.

Zoé still made the decisions. She still applied judgement. She still owned the outcomes.

Her days flowed.

Once she experienced that shift, she realised something important: AI wasn't about doing more for its own sake. It was about creating space for focus, creativity, and better thinking—where life actually happens.

> *This fictional story introduces the themes of **Part 3**.*

16

AI for Personal Productivity

A New Kind of Personal Assistant

Now that you have explored how humans and AI complement each other, we shift into the spaces where this partnership becomes most visible: your everyday routines. Productivity is not about doing more—it is about removing the friction that slows you down. AI excels at this. It turns scattered thoughts into plans, overwhelming information into clarity, and time-consuming tasks into quick actions. This chapter focuses on practical ways AI can simplify your day and help you operate with greater confidence and ease.

Turning Tasks into Actionable Plans

From overwhelming lists to a clear structure

Most to-do lists grow faster than they shrink. They become a jumble of ideas, obligations, and half-finished plans. AI can take that chaos and turn it into a prioritised, organised plan. You can paste a messy list into an AI tool, and the AI will group items, order them intelligently, highlight what matters most, and even suggest realistic timelines. Suddenly, the day becomes manageable rather than stressful.

Breaking big tasks into simple steps

Large tasks often feel intimidating because they lack structure. Ask AI to break a project into steps, assign milestones, or outline a realistic schedule. It helps you see the path forward, not just the weight of the work. Instead of asking, *"Where do I start?"* you move forward with clarity.

Sample Prompt:

> "Following is my to-do task list. Please organise these tasks into categories, prioritise them, estimate how long each might take, and create a realistic, step-by-step plan for my day. Also, highlight which tasks require deep focus and which ones are quick wins.
>
> *My tasks:*
> - Prepare slides for tomorrow's meeting
> - Finish the monthly report
> - Respond to Sarah's email
> - Plan meals for the week
> - Research new software tools"

Managing Information Without Overwhelm

Summaries That Save Time and Energy

Emails, articles, reports, messages—digital life produces more information than anyone can reasonably absorb. AI helps by summarising long content into what actually matters: key points, decisions, insights, or action items. You stay informed without being overwhelmed by the details.

Extracting Meaning from Complexity

Beyond summarising, AI can simplify technical documents, extract themes from text, compare viewpoints, or convert dense writing into plain language. This turns difficult material into something you can understand and act upon quickly.

Sample Prompt:

> "Please summarise the following text into the most important points I need to understand. Include key decisions, deadlines, risks, and any actions required from me. Keep the summary clear and concise.
>
> *Text:* During today's meeting, the finance team confirmed that Q2 budgeting must be finalised by April 5. Departments need to submit revised expense forecasts by March 28. A decision is still pending on whether to allocate extra budget to customer support for the new onboarding tool. There is a risk that if the forecasts are submitted late, the financial review committee will not have sufficient time to approve adjustments before the April 5 cut-off. Action required: Please review your department's forecast and submit any updates by March 28. Additionally, please share your recommendation on the proposed budget increase for customer support so it can be included in the committee's discussion."

Communicating Clearly and Confidently

Drafting Messages with Ease

Writing is a significant productivity bottleneck. Be it an email, a request, a proposal, or a sensitive message, finding the right words can take longer than expected. AI helps you draft the first version quickly and refine it to match your voice and tone.

Polishing Your Ideas into A Clear Expression

Sometimes you know what you want to say, but struggle to express it. AI can reorganise your thoughts, adjust the tone, reduce repetition, and make the message smoother and more effective—while still sounding like *you*.

Sample Prompt

> "Please rewrite the following message to sound clear, professional, and polite, while keeping my original meaning. Provide two versions: one formal and one friendly.
>
> *Message:* Hi Sarah, I'm not sure what you meant in the last part of your email. Can you explain it again?"

Planning Your Day, Week, and Projects

Turning Vague Intentions into Concrete Plans

Planning is easier when you do not have to do it alone. Whether you are preparing for a meeting, organising a trip, setting long-term goals, or launching a personal project, AI helps you turn scattered ideas into structured plans with clear next steps.

Exploring Multiple Paths Before Choosing One

AI can offer several possible approaches to a project, proposal, or schedule you are considering. It acts as an impartial adviser, revealing options and perspectives you might have missed. This makes your decision-making more thoughtful and less rushed.

Sample Prompt

> "Please create a structured weekly plan based on the items below. Group them by category, assign suggested days, identify tasks requiring deep focus, and highlight items that can be batched together. Also, prepare a summary of my priorities for the week.
>
> *Tasks for the week:*
> - Prepare monthly budget
> - Team meeting on Wednesday
> - Finish project proposal
> - Gym three times
> - Grocery shopping
> - Research new software tools
> - Family lunch on Sunday
> - Update LinkedIn profile
> - Review supplier contracts"

Using AI as a Thinking Partner

Reflecting with Greater Clarity

When faced with a difficult decision, a confusing situation, or a problem that does not have an obvious solution, AI can help you reason through it. You can ask it to break down trade-offs, highlight risks, or offer multiple perspectives. It does not decide for you—but it helps you think more clearly.

Understanding Patterns in Your Habits or Work

AI can help you analyse your routines, identify where your time goes, or reveal patterns in your behaviour. This makes personal improvement more intentional and grounded in real insight.

Sample Prompt:

> "I'd like your help thinking through a situation. Please identify the key factors I should consider, outline several possible options, list the pros and cons of each, and indicate any blind spots or risks I may be missing.
>
> *Here is the situation*: I'm feeling burnt out, but I'm not sure whether I should take time off, reduce my workload, or push through. I'm worried about falling behind, yet I also know that continuing like this might make things worse."

Small Everyday Tasks That Create Big Savings

The Little Tasks That Quietly Drain Your Time

AI is surprisingly effective at handling the small, everyday tasks that accumulate throughout the week, from drafting shopping lists and creating reminders to converting handwritten notes into structured lists, rewriting instructions, or planning simple meals. These small efficiencies compound over time, freeing your mind for things that truly matter.

Sample Prompt:

> "Please create a clean, organised shopping list based on the notes below. Group items into logical categories (e.g., fresh produce, household items, pantry staples), highlight anything essential I may have missed, and keep the list simple and practical.
>
> *Notes:*
> - Need vegetables
> - Running low on rice
> - Almost out of toothpaste
> - Want ingredients for spaghetti
> - Snacks for the kids
> - Cleaning spray"

The Real Power of AI in Productivity

AI Reduces Friction, So You Can Focus on What Matters

The most valuable impact of AI is not that it works quickly; it is that it removes the mental friction that slows you down. When writing is easier, planning is clearer, decisions are less overwhelming, and information is more digestible, your mind relaxes. You can do better work not because you work harder, but because the path is smoother.

A Partner, Not A Replacement

AI does not eliminate the need for human judgement—in fact, it increases the need for it. Instead, it amplifies your ability to stay organised, communicate effectively, think deeply, and act with clarity. The more you integrate AI into your routines, the more you will experience this sense of momentum and ease.

* * *

This chapter introduced the groundwork for using AI to improve your personal productivity. In the next chapter, we shift into your professional world: how AI can accelerate your learning, elevate your work, enhance your communication, and strengthen your career. Personal and professional productivity often overlap, and once you have mastered the self-management side, the workplace benefits become even more powerful.

17

AI for Work and Career Growth

The workplace is one of the clearest arenas where AI's strengths become immediately visible. While the previous chapter explained how AI can simplify your personal life, this chapter expands the lens to the professional world, where clarity, communication, and continuous learning are crucial daily. AI can accelerate your career growth by helping you learn faster, express ideas more clearly, and handle complex tasks with far less friction. This chapter explores how AI is not only a tool but a catalyst for career growth.

Learning Faster: AI as Your Personal Mentor

In today's world, almost every profession requires constant learning—new tools, new systems, new trends, new expectations. What often slows people down is not the content itself, but the time required to process it. AI shortens that distance dramatically by adapting explanations to your level and learning style.

You can ask AI to explain a concept in simple terms, break down a technical idea, provide examples relevant to your industry, or compare two ideas you are struggling to differentiate. It can generate quizzes, flashcards, summaries, checklists, or step-by-step learning plans tailored to your pace. If you are trying to learn something complex, you can ask the model to explain it like a mentor would—starting broad, filling gaps in your understanding, and gradually increasing depth.

One of the most valuable learning techniques is to ask AI to assess your understanding. You can describe what you know, and the model will point out missing pieces, clarify misconceptions, and help you refine your mental model. This turns passive reading into active learning. Over time, you build confidence not just because you know more, but because you understand the structure of the knowledge itself.

Sample Prompt:

> "I'm trying to learn a new concept and would like you to act as a personal mentor. Please explain it in simple terms, giving a real-life example, and then check my understanding by asking three questions. After answering, correct any misunderstandings and provide a deeper explanation.
>
> *The concept I want to learn is*: What is cloud computing, and why do businesses use it?"

Improving Communication: Clearer Writing, Better Thinking

Communication is one of the most essential skills in any career, and also one of the most time-consuming. Professionals spend a significant portion of their day writing emails, documenting decisions, preparing updates, responding to stakeholders, or explaining complex ideas. AI helps by transforming raw thoughts into polished, professional communication.

You can dictate rough ideas, paste a messy paragraph, or outline the key points you want to convey. AI will help you refine the structure, adjust the tone, remove redundancy, and ensure clarity. It can make your writing formal when needed, conversational when appropriate, or neutral when the situation is sensitive. This reduces the time you spend agonising over phrasing while improving your overall communication quality.

AI is especially helpful when the message is tough, delivering feedback, asking for clarity, declining a request, or navigating conflict. It helps you express yourself clearly while maintaining professionalism and empathy. Over time, your own communication skills improve because the model exposes you to clearer ways of expressing ideas.

Sample Prompt:

> "I need help expressing my idea clearly and professionally. Please take the draft below and do the following:
> – Identify the core message I'm trying to communicate.
> – Rewrite it in a clear, concise, and polished way.
> – Present two versions with distinct tones: professional and friendly.
> – Suggest an improvement to my argument or structure for the message to be stronger.
>
> *Here is my draft*: I think we may need to rethink the project timeline because things are getting complicated and we might not finish on time."

Presentation and Report Assistance: Turning Ideas Into Professional Outputs

Many people have strong ideas but struggle to present them clearly in slides, reports, or briefs. AI helps translate your thinking into structured, polished output that is ready for meetings or stakeholder discussions.

You can paste your notes and ask AI to turn them into a presentation outline, complete with headings, key points, and suggested visuals. It can create executive summaries, detailed explanations, comparison tables, or recommendation sections tailored to your audience. If you are preparing a report, AI can help refine arguments, strengthen transitions, and ensure that the structure follows a logical flow.

This support is not about outsourcing your thinking—it is about removing the bottleneck between the idea in your mind and the deliverable on your screen. When the formatting, structuring, and polishing happen more quickly, you gain more time to focus on insights and strategy.

Sample Prompt:

> "Act as an experienced Project Manager and turn the notes below into a clear, professional presentation outline.
>
> *Please do the following:*
> - Identify the main message and propose a logical structure.
> - Create slide headings with 2–3 bullet points under each.
> - Suggest one visual or chart that would strengthen the presentation.
> - Provide a one-paragraph executive summary I can include in a report.

> *My notes:* The team is behind on deadlines, not because of a lack of effort, but because the requirements are not well defined. Communication gaps between departments cause rework. We need a clearer workflow, stronger documentation, and weekly alignment meetings."

Skill-Building With AI: Growing Your Career Faster

AI is not only a tool for completing tasks—it is a partner for expanding your abilities. You can use it to strengthen almost any professional skill, from writing and reasoning to technical understanding and leadership.

If you want to improve at problem-solving, you can ask AI to create scenarios that challenge your thinking. If you are looking to strengthen your industry knowledge, AI can also summarise trends, explain terminology, or outline frameworks used by experts in your field. If you are developing leadership skills, you can use AI to practise difficult conversations, generate coaching questions, or rewrite feedback more constructively.

AI also helps you break down large skill areas into achievable steps. If you want to learn project management, data analysis, user experience design, or strategic planning, you can ask the model to map the learning journey. You will then be guided on where to begin, how the concepts connect, which resources to use, and how long each stage is likely to take. This gives you a sense of direction and measurable progress.

Perhaps most importantly, AI lowers the barrier to starting something new. You no longer need to wait for a formal course or expert guidance. You can begin exploring immediately, supported by a system that adapts to your pace and curiosity.

Sample Prompt:

> "Assume the role of a career development coach. I want to build a new professional skill, and I need a clear learning plan.
>
> *Please perform the following steps*:
> - Break the skill into key sub-skills I need to master.
> - Create a step-by-step 4-week learning plan.
> - Suggest practical exercises I can complete each week.
> - Explain how this skill applies in real workplace scenarios.
>
> *The skill I want to develop is*: Data analysis for business decision-making."

Career Transformation Stories: How AI Elevates Real People

To appreciate AI's greatest impact on career growth, it's helpful to explore how everyday people are using these tools to transition into new roles, accelerate their development, and overcome long-standing barriers.

Jane, a marketing professional, struggled with data analysis. Previously, understanding metrics required constant help from analysts. With AI, she now generates quick insights, summarises dashboards, and prepares reports independently, allowing her to contribute more strategically. She did not become a data scientist, but she became more capable in her role.

John, a teacher, uses AI to draft lesson plans, create worksheets, and summarise educational research. Instead of spending hours preparing materials, he focuses on personalising learning for his students. AI did not replace him; it amplified him.

Emma is returning to the workforce after a long break. With AI as a tutor, she learned updated workplace tools, practised interview skills, rewrote her CV, and built confidence. Acting as a personalised coach, AI helped her re-enter the job market with confidence.

There are also numerous stories of entrepreneurs using AI to invent ideas, test concepts, build websites, automate administrative work, and produce marketing materials. AI becomes an innovation partner, allowing people to launch projects that once felt out of reach.

These examples reveal a simple truth: *AI does not transform your career on its own—it transforms what you can do.* It expands your capacity, deepens your understanding, and accelerates your growth, allowing you to achieve more with the time and skills you already possess.

Sample Prompt:

> "Act as my AI marketing analyst and help me build confidence in interpreting campaign metrics and drawing meaningful insights independently.
>
> Using the example metrics below, walk me through what they mean, what story the data is telling, and what decisions a strong marketer would make from them.
>
> Then create a learning plan that indicates what I should master next (e.g., attribution, segmentation, forecasting) and how I can use AI tools to refine these skills with ease.
>
> *Example metrics:*
> – CTR dropped from 3.2% to 1.8%
> – CPC increased by 25%
> – Conversions stable
> – Bounce rate high on mobile"

* * *

When you use AI to learn faster, communicate clearly, present persuasively, and build skills with purpose, your career gains momentum that feels natural and sustainable. The more you collaborate with AI, the more capable you become—and the more confident you feel navigating new challenges.

In the next chapter, we turn to *business* and *entrepreneurship*, where AI becomes not just a personal asset but a strategic advantage—helping you to work smarter, innovate faster, and make better decisions.

18

AI in Business and Entrepreneurship

Modern AI helps businesses move faster, think more clearly, and compete more effectively. AI is no longer a luxury reserved for large corporations with specialist teams. Today, even a solo entrepreneur or a small business owner can access tools that analyse markets, generate content, automate support, and manage sales pipelines—all without writing a single line of code. This chapter shows you where AI delivers the greatest value in business, and how you can turn it into a practical advantage, not a theoretical concept.

AI in Marketing: Reach the Right People With Less Effort

Marketing used to rely heavily on manual research, guesswork, and slow experimentation. Today, AI transforms this landscape by analysing customer behaviour, generating content, and optimising campaigns at scale—even for small teams.

AI tools can help:

- Analyse audience behaviour and interests
- Identify high-performing keywords or content topics
- Write effective adverts, landing pages, captions, and emails
- Repurpose one idea into dozens of assets

- Predict which messages will resonate with specific customer segments

This is particularly powerful for entrepreneurs who juggle multiple roles. Instead of drowning under a constant demand for content, you can use AI as your creative support system—turning raw ideas into polished output that reflects your brand.

Sample Prompt:

> "Act as my AI marketing strategist. I want to refine my audience targeting and improve engagement across my marketing channels.
>
> Analyse the customer profile and product details below, identify the audience segments most likely to respond, and recommend messaging themes, content angles, and the platforms where these audiences are most active.
>
> Then create a weekly content plan with 10 tailored post ideas.
>
> *Customer profile:*
> – Young professionals aged 25–40
> – Interested in productivity, self-improvement, and career growth
> – Tech-savvy but time-constrained
> – Prefer clear, actionable content that helps them achieve quick wins
>
> *Product details:* A subscription-based productivity app that uses AI to help users plan their day, manage tasks, and stay focused.
>
> *Current challenges:*
> – Low engagement on social media

> – Messaging feels too generic and not aligned with audience needs
> – Difficulty identifying the most effective channels
> – Not enough clarity on what content resonates most
>
> Generate the full analysis and content plan."

AI in Sales: Smarter Insights, Faster Closes

Sales is not only about persuasion; it is about understanding customer needs, following up consistently, and communicating clearly. AI supports this by extracting insights from conversations, drafting personalised follow-ups, and helping you keep track of opportunities.

AI tools can:

- Summarise sales calls and highlight customer objections
- Draft follow-up emails tailored to each customer
- Predict which leads are likely to convert
- Create personalised proposals and pitch decks
- Help sales teams prepare for meetings by analysing previous interactions

This is transformative for growing businesses because it ensures every lead gets the proper attention—without the founder or sales team burning out.

Sample Prompt:

> "Act as my AI sales analyst. I want to understand how to improve my sales conversations and close deals more effectively.
>
> Using the sample call notes below, identify the client's real needs,

objections, buying signals, and potential risks.

Then recommend the best follow-up message, key talking points for the next call, and a short action plan to move this deal forward.

Sample call notes:
- The client is struggling with workflow automation
- Interested in reducing manual admin work
- Concerned about cost and implementation time
- Wants to see a quick win within the first month
- Asked about integrations with existing tools
- Said their team is overwhelmed but open to trying new solutions

My goals:
- Address concerns clearly
- Show strong value quickly
- Increase the chance of closing within 2–3 weeks

Provide a structured analysis, recommended follow-up email, and next-step plan."

AI in Customer Service: Faster Response, Higher Satisfaction

Customers today expect quick, accurate, and polite responses. AI helps businesses meet these expectations without expanding support teams. Well-designed AI workflows can respond instantly, provide troubleshooting steps, draft replies for human agents, and escalate only the complex cases.

AI can support customer service by:

- Producing consistent, helpful responses
- Summarising customer issues from long messages

- Categorising support tickets
- Identifying recurring problems in customer feedback
- Automating simple resolutions, such as refunds or password resets

Sample Prompt:

> "Be my AI customer support specialist. I want to boost the speed, clarity, and consistency of our customer service responses.
>
> Using the customer message below, summarise the issue, classify the type of request, identify the customer's underlying concern, and draft a professional, empathetic response that follows best-practice support standards.
>
> Then suggest how the issue could be prevented in future and provide a template we can reuse for similar cases.
>
> *Customer message:* Hi, I signed up for your premium plan last month, but I'm still seeing a message saying my account is on the free tier. I've tried logging out and back in, but nothing changed. Can you please help? I'm worried my payment didn't go through.
>
> *My goals:*
> – Reduce response time
> – Improve clarity and empathy in replies
> – Avoid inconsistency between different support agents
> – Create reusable templates for recurring issues
>
> *Provide:*
> – Issue summary
> – Request category
> – Underlying concern

> – Draft response
> – Preventative suggestion
> – Reusable template"

AI for Business Planning: Turning Ideas into Actionable Strategies

Business planning often feels overwhelming: market sizing, competitive analysis, revenue forecasting, pricing, and positioning all require careful thought process. AI can dramatically accelerate these steps by helping you clarify your vision and test the logic of your ideas.

AI can help:

- Draft business plans, pitch decks, and executive summaries
- Identify potential customer segments and value propositions
- Estimate costs and revenue scenarios
- Break large ideas into clear roadmaps
- Create alternative versions of your strategy for comparison

The goal is not to let AI make the decisions for you, but to use it as a thought partner — challenging your assumptions, extending your analysis, and revealing blind spots.

Sample Prompt:

> "Act as my AI business strategist. I want to turn my business idea into a clear and actionable plan.
>
> Using the idea described below, identify the target customers, the core value proposition, potential revenue streams, key risks, and the steps required to launch.

> Then create a simple 12-month roadmap divided into phases, with milestones for each stage.
>
> *Business idea:* A mobile app that helps freelancers track their time, create invoices automatically, and receive personalised insights on improving their earning patterns.
>
> *My goals:*
> - Understand who the real customers are
> - Clarify how this product delivers value
> - Explore pricing and revenue models
> - See a realistic launch pathway
> - Identify major risks early
>
> *Provide:*
> - Customer segmentation
> - Clear value proposition
> - Revenue stream options
> - Key risks and risk-reduction strategies
> - A 12-month roadmap with milestones
> - A concise one-page business summary"

AI for Market Research: Insights Without the Overwhelm

Traditional market research is slow and expensive. AI compresses this process into minutes by scanning public data, competitor websites, product reviews, and online conversations. It won't replace a professional analyst entirely, but it can give small businesses a strong starting point.

AI can help you:

- Identify customer pain points
- Compare competitor offerings
- Analyse product reviews for recurring themes
- Extract insights from large datasets or surveys
- Explore untapped market opportunities

Instead of spending weeks compiling information, you can move faster and make decisions with greater confidence.

Sample Prompt:

> "Act in the role of my AI market research analyst. I want to understand my market, competitors, and customer needs without spending weeks gathering information.
>
> Using the product description below, identify the ideal customer segments, their pain points, and what motivates them to buy.
>
> Then analyse my top competitors, highlight gaps I can exploit, and summarise current trends in the industry.
>
> Finally, turn everything into a concise set of insights I can use for planning and marketing.
>
> *Product:* A subscription-based platform that teaches small businesses how to use AI tools for marketing, automation, and content creation.
>
> *My goals:*
> – Understand who needs this product most
> – Identify the problems customers are trying to solve
> – See how competitors position themselves

> – Spot opportunities or unmet demand
> – Get a clear strategic summary I can act on
>
> *Please provide:*
> – Customer segmentation
> – Pain points and buying motivations
> – Competitor overview and gaps
> – Industry trends
> – Opportunities worth exploring
> – A short 'What this means for your business' summary."

AI for Content Generation: From Ideas to Polished Output

Every business communicates through digital platforms, emails, newsletters, blogs, presentations, and social media. AI makes this workload manageable, even if writing is not your strength.

AI can:

- Generate blog posts, email newsletters, and social captions
- Rewrite content to suit different tones
- Convert one article into multiple formats
- Edit, proofread, and improve clarity
- Create product descriptions, scripts, and storyboards

For entrepreneurs who struggle to maintain a consistent content stream, AI is a game-changer. With clear prompts and a solid sense of your brand voice, you can produce more high-quality content in less time.

Sample Prompt:

"Assume the role of an AI content strategist and writer. My goal is to transform the initial ideas listed below into polished, engaging content that aligns with my brand voice.

First, refine the ideas and suggest the strongest angles for my audience.

Then create a structured outline for each piece, followed by a polished draft in a clear and professional tone.

Brand voice:

- Professional but friendly
- Confident, clear, and easy to understand
- Practical and solution-focused
- Avoids jargon unless necessary
- Encouraging and empowering

Initial ideas:

- How small businesses can automate admin tasks
- The benefits of AI-powered customer support
- Common productivity mistakes entrepreneurs make
- Why content consistency matters for brand trust

My goals:

- Improve the quality and clarity of my content
- Save time on drafting and editing
- Ensure all content speaks directly to my audience's needs
- Generate material I can use across blogs, emails, and social platforms

Please provide:

> – Improved ideas and angles
> – An outline for each topic
> – One polished, ready-to-publish draft written in my brand voice
> – Suggestions for repurposing the content across different platforms."

* * *

AI does not replace entrepreneurial spirit—it amplifies it. It gives individuals and small businesses the power to analyse markets, generate content, create strategies, and engage customers with a level of speed and sophistication that once required entire teams. The goal is not to let AI run your business, but to let it clear the path so you can focus on the decisions, relationships, and creativity that truly matter.

19

AI for Creativity

Creativity has never been a rare gift reserved for a few; it is a process—exploration, experimentation, and a willingness to play with ideas. What has changed is that AI can now join that process. It can help overcome creative blocks, suggest new styles, and shape rough concepts into polished work. AI can collaborate with you to craft stories, design visuals, compose music, and express ideas more vividly.

AI does not replace your imagination; it expands it. The tools introduced in this chapter demonstrate how generative systems work, how to use them effectively, and what responsible creativity looks like in an age where machines can produce ideas and art almost as quickly as we can think them.

Creativity Across Media: Writing, Art, Design and Music

AI for Writing: From Ideas to Drafts to Refined Prose

Writers often experience the same challenges: staring at a blank page, struggling to find the right phrasing, or attempting to structure an idea that still feels unformed. AI smooths this process by acting as a brainstorming partner, editor, and co-writer—depending on what you need in the moment.

You can use AI to:

- brainstorm topics and storylines
- generate outlines that give structure before drafting
- rewrite or refine text for tone, clarity, and flow
- explore alternative voices or perspectives
- break long-form writing into digestible sections

The key is not to let AI write for you, but to let it accelerate the parts that slow you down so that your own creativity has more space to flourish.

AI for Art: Imagery, Style, and Visual Exploration

Visual creativity has become dramatically more accessible. With a short description, AI can produce sketches, illustrations, photorealistic images, or artworks inspired by specific styles. This is incredibly useful for anyone who needs visuals—marketers, educators, designers, or entrepreneurs — even if they do not have formal art training.

AI can help you:

- generate mood boards
- try different artistic styles
- convert simple drawings into detailed scenes
- visualise concepts that are difficult to describe
- iterate rapidly until you land on something compelling

You remain the creative director; AI only provides the variations.

AI for Design: Layouts, Branding and User Experience

Modern design is a balance of aesthetics and function. AI tools now support by suggesting layouts, colour palettes, typography combinations, and even wireframes for apps or websites. Designers no longer need to start from scratch—they can begin from AI-generated concepts and refine them with their own judgement.

AI supports designers by:

- producing fast concept prototypes
- analysing visual balance and readability
- generating multiple brand identity options
- refining UX flows based on common patterns
- assisting with accessible design choices

This reduces time spent on early experimentation and increases time for deliberate, thoughtful design.

AI for Music: Ideas, Rhythm, and Creative Expansion

AI-driven music tools can generate melodies, harmonies, rhythms, and even entire compositions. They are helpful for creators who have strong conceptual ideas but limited musical training, allowing them to experiment with sound in ways that would otherwise be inaccessible.

AI can support your musical creativity through:

- generating variations on a melody
- creating backing tracks in specific genres
- suggesting chord progressions
- remixing a simple idea into multiple styles
- helping you construct a full arrangement

The magic lies in using AI as a musical sketchbook—a space to explore sound without friction.

Ethics of Creative AI: Responsibility in the New Creative Landscape

As AI becomes more involved in creative work, ethical questions naturally arise. Creativity covers culture, identity, intellectual property, and community—so responsible use is crucial.

Copyright and Originality

Generative AI is trained on enormous datasets that include copyrighted works. While AI does not "copy" those works directly, it can reproduce styles or patterns in ways that raise valid concerns. Creators should avoid using AI to mimic the style of specific artists without permission, especially for commercial purposes.

Transparency

When AI contributes significantly to a creative work, audiences deserve clarity. Whether you're designing a marketing graphic or generating lyrics, transparency builds trust and prevents misunderstandings.

Authenticity and Voice

AI can accelerate your output, but your unique perspective is irreplaceable. The best creative work comes from a blend of human intention and machine assistance—not from relying on AI to generate everything.

Bias and Representation

Generative models may reflect societal biases present in their training data. When creating characters, images, or stories with AI, it is important to check for unintended stereotypes or imbalances.

Impact on Creative Industries

AI will change creative professions, but it does not eliminate the need for human vision. Instead, it shifts the focus toward directing, curating, editing, and shaping ideas. Those who embrace AI as a tool, not a threat, gain a competitive edge.

Try-It-Yourself—Creative Exercises

To help you experience AI creativity first-hand, the guided exercises below are designed to build your confidence and spark your inspiration.

Exercise 1—Turning a Blank Page into Ideas (Writing)

> *Prompt:* "Give me five opening paragraphs for a story about someone discovering a hidden ability, each in a different tone: suspenseful, humorous, poetic, dramatic, and reflective."
>
> *Goal:* Understand how style shifts tone and mood.

Exercise 2—Visual Exploration (Art and Design)

> *Prompt:* "Create three concept sketches of a futuristic workspace: a minimalist version, a nature-inspired one, and a third that is imaginative and surreal."
>
> *Goal:* See how AI interprets style, structure, and atmosphere.

Exercise 3—Style Transfer for Branding

> *Prompt:* "Generate three logo concepts for a small bakery called 'Golden Crust', each using a different design direction: elegant, playful, and rustic."
>
> *Goal:* Quickly explore variations of your brand identity.

Exercise 4—Musical Variation

> *Prompt:* "Create three variations of a simple four-note melody: upbeat and fast, calm and atmospheric, and dramatic and cinematic."
>
> *Goal:* Experience how AI transforms musical ideas across genres.

Exercise 5—Multimodal Creativity Challenge

> *Prompt:* "Based on the sentence 'The city woke to a sky streaked with gold,' generate a visual, a short musical theme, and a paragraph that captures the same mood."
>
> *Goal:* See how AI connects concepts across different creative mediums.

* * *

Ideas that once required technical skill, specialised equipment, or years of practice can now be explored instantly. The role of the human creator becomes even more powerful: to decide what matters, what feels authentic, and what direction to explore next. AI becomes the collaborator who brings possibilities to life at the speed of imagination.

20

AI for Learning, Teaching and Decision-Making

Learning has always been a deeply human activity—a mix of curiosity, effort, confusion, insight, and gradual progress. What has changed is that AI now acts as a companion within that journey. It can clarify difficult concepts, generate practice questions, organise study plans, evaluate drafts, and help you reason through complicated decisions. For teachers, it lightens the administrative load and expands the range of support they can give their students. This chapter explores how AI supports learning, teaching, and thoughtful decision-making without replacing the essential role of human judgement.

AI As a Personal Tutor

Everyone learns differently. Some people prefer clear explanations; others need examples, visuals, or step-by-step breakdowns. Traditional education rarely adapts to individual needs—but AI does.

Tailored Explanations at the Right Level

An AI tutor can adjust to your knowledge level instantly. If you ask for a simple explanation of a topic, it can start with a beginner-friendly overview. If you already know the basics, it can raise the difficulty and build on what you understand. This adaptability makes the learning experience smoother and less frustrating.

Lesson Plans and Structured Paths

AI can take a broad goal—such as learning Python, improving writing, or preparing for an exam—and convert it into a structured learning path. It can break complex subjects into manageable stages, estimate how long each stage might take, and provide practice exercises for reinforcement.

Study Guides and Practice Questions

Instead of spending hours creating your own revision materials, you can ask AI to summarise chapters, generate practice questions, explain past exam mistakes, or create flashcards. It becomes easier to move from passive reading to active learning.

Clarifying Confusion Instantly

A major advantage of AI tutoring is immediacy. When you encounter a sentence, formula, or concept that does not make sense, you can ask for clarification instantly—without waiting for a teacher, tutor, or class session. This keeps your momentum intact.

Teaching With AI

Teachers handle an enormous amount of work, including planning lessons, grading, answering questions, providing feedback, creating differentiated materials, and adapting lessons for varied learning abilities. AI supports them in the areas that consume time and energy.

Lesson Planning and Curriculum Support

AI can help teachers design lesson plans aligning with learning objectives, create extension tasks for advanced students, and differentiate content for those who need extra support. By generating alternative explanations or examples, AI enables teachers to cater for all learners with different needs.

Feedback on Student Work

Instead of manually correcting every minor error in writing or problem-solving steps, teachers can use AI to provide preliminary feedback. The teacher still has the final say, but the AI highlights key insights into student work, such as common mistakes, missing reasoning steps, or unclear arguments. This narrows the teacher's focus to the areas where human insight is most needed.

Creating Classroom Materials

AI can generate worksheets, quiz questions, reading passages, case studies, and discussion prompts. This frees teachers to spend more time engaging with students rather than creating resources from scratch.

Supporting Diverse Learners

Students learn in different ways—through visuals, analogies, or step-by-step reasoning. AI can instantly produce materials in multiple formats, providing teachers with flexible tools to support diverse learning styles.

AI for Judgement and Decision Support

Good decisions rely on clear thinking, not speed. But real-life decisions often feel tangled—too many variables, incomplete information, conflicting priorities, and emotional pressure. AI cannot *make* decisions for you, but it can help you organise your thinking so that the path forward becomes clearer.

Structuring Complex Problems

One of AI's greatest strengths is its ability to organise messy information. You can describe a decision you are struggling with—be it personal or professional—and ask AI to break it into components: goals, options, risks, assumptions, trade-offs, and unknowns. Seeing the pieces laid out makes the situation more manageable.

Revealing Hidden Assumptions

AI can challenge your reasoning by identifying assumptions you never realised you were making. It can ask clarifying questions, suggest alternative viewpoints, and highlight where emotion might be clouding judgement. This strengthens your decision-making process without dictating the final choice.

Scenario Planning and Consequence Mapping

AI can help you envision how different decisions might unfold. For example, if you are considering a career change, it can outline the short-term and long-term implications, risks, and opportunities of each route. This type of structured foresight helps you make proactive rather than reactive choices.

Reducing Cognitive Load

Humans can only hold a limited number of variables in their working memory. AI can externalise that load by tracking details, comparing options, or generating summaries. You are still the one making the call, but the thinking becomes clearer and more structured.

Multiple-Perspective Thinking

One of the most underrated uses of AI is its ability to generate perspectives you might not naturally consider. This is particularly powerful in situations where bias, habit, or narrow framing limit your thinking.

Considering Stakeholder Views

If you are making a decision that affects others—colleagues, customers, students, or family members—AI can help you imagine how each group might experience the outcome. This strengthens empathy and reveals consequences you may not have anticipated.

Exploring Alternative Framings

The way you frame a problem shapes the solution you find. AI can reframe a situation through strategic, emotional, operational, and ethical perspectives, providing a deeper understanding of the underlying issue.

Challenging Your Default Approach

AI can identify cognitive biases such as confirmation bias, anchoring, and overconfidence. By prompting you to consider contrasting viewpoints, it helps reduce blind spots.

Strengthening Critical Thinking

Seeing multiple angles encourages more rigorous reasoning. The goal is not to overwhelm you with options but to ensure that your preferred choice is considered and grounded.

* * *

AI's role in learning, teaching, and decision-making expands your ability to understand new concepts, helps educators reach more students with less strain, and adds clarity to difficult decisions. In every case, the value of AI comes from its partnership with human judgement—not from operating independently. When used thoughtfully, AI becomes a tool that enhances our capacity to think, learn, and lead with confidence.

IV

PART 4—Using AI for Technical Work, Demystified

Part 4 takes you into the technical side of AI—without assuming any technical background. We break down concepts like coding assistants, data analysis, APIs, and automation in plain language, showing how they work and how to use them right away. Each chapter turns what once felt complicated into clear, practical steps you can understand and apply with confidence.

21

A Short Story: When the Pieces Finally Connected

Theodore had always believed that "technical" meant complicated.

He associated it with dense documentation, unfamiliar terms, and the quiet assumption that you either had the background or you did not. For years, he worked around technical systems rather than with them, relying on specialists whenever something crossed an invisible line.

AI disrupted that belief.

At first, he used it cautiously. He asked it to explain a piece of code he did not fully understand, then to help clean a messy dataset, and eventually to automate a small task he repeated every week.

Nothing broke. In fact, the pieces began to fall into place.

The coding assistant not only generated snippets; it explained why they worked. When something failed, it suggested alternatives. When Theodore hesitated, it provided structure. Syntax stopped being the barrier it once was.

Encouraged, he went further.

He used AI to analyse data that had previously felt intimidating, asking questions in plain language and watching patterns emerge—summaries, trends, anomalies—without writing complex queries. What once took hours of trial and error became a conversation.

Then came the systems.

Theodore discovered that AI could connect to other tools, call external services, retrieve information from documents, and search vast collections of data by meaning rather than keywords. He did not need to understand every technical detail—only what each part was responsible for. It came down to three essentials: the inputs that shape the request, the outputs that deliver the result, and the flow that connects them.

The real shift emerged when his focus shifted from individual tasks to end-to-end workflows. One step triggered the next. Information moved. Decisions followed. The system adjusted as it went.

It felt less like programming and more like designing a process.

What surprised Theodore most was that he had not crossed into "technical" territory as he once imagined it. He had not memorised frameworks or mastered jargon; he had learned how the pieces fit together—and that was enough.

By the end, he was not only using AI tools; he was building with them—carefully, intentionally, and with growing confidence.

What once felt like a sealed world had opened—not because it had become simpler, but because it was finally explained in a way that made sense.

This fictional story introduces the themes of ***Part 4****.*

22

AI in Software Development

For many people, software development feels like a domain reserved for specialists—something complex, technical, and inaccessible. Yet AI has quietly transformed the craft of programming into something far more approachable. Developers at all levels, from beginners to senior engineers, now work side-by-side with AI systems that help them write, understand, and maintain code. These tools do not replace human judgement or creativity; instead, they enhance it.

In this chapter, you will learn how AI copilots assist with coding tasks, how code generation works, how debugging becomes more efficient, and how documentation almost writes itself. You will also go through a simple step-by-step example to see the workflow in action. Whether you code every day or you are just curious about how AI is changing the industry, this chapter gives you a clear picture of how software development now happens in practice.

Copilots—Your AI Assistant in the Editor

AI copilots are tools that run inside a coding environment, such as GitHub Copilot in VS Code and JetBrains AI Assistant in JetBrains IDEs. There are also platform-independent assistants such as GitLab Duo, Codeium, and AWS CodeWhisperer that work across multiple editors and interfaces. These tools provide real-time support as code is being written. They can be understood as very advanced autocomplete systems that recognise context, style, and intent and can suggest full lines or sections of code rather than just individual characters.

Apart from IDE-integrated copilots, general AI models like OpenAI ChatGPT or Meta AI can also assist with coding tasks. These tools are not considered copilots because they do not operate inside the coding environment. Instead, they act as general-purpose AI coding assistants that help through conversation rather than real-time code suggestions.

The word "copilot" originated from aviation, where the copilot assists the main pilot during flight. GitHub popularised the term in the AI world with GitHub Copilot, and it has since become a widely used metaphor for AI systems that support, but do not replace, human work.

What Copilots Do Well

- Predict your next line of code based on patterns in your file
- Generate functions you describe in plain language
- Suggest alternative approaches or optimisations
- Fill in repetitive boilerplate code
- Explain unfamiliar code in simple, readable terms
- Assist with troubleshooting by identifying errors, suggesting fixes, and explaining likely causes
- Generate unit tests that validate expected behaviour and edge cases
- Produce clear documentation and comments from existing code
- Translate code between programming languages while preserving intent and logic

Why Copilots Matter

Before AI copilots, developers spent a lot of time:

- searching Stack Overflow
- reading documentation
- copying patterns from older projects
- writing repetitive setup code

Now, much of this "overhead" is handled automatically. Copilots make the work feel more fluid—less about fighting syntax and more about solving problems.

A Key Mindset

A copilot is *not* an authority; it is a collaborator. You accept good suggestions, reject poor ones, and use your judgement to steer the solution. You remain fully in control.

Code Generation—Turning Plain Language into Working Code

One of the greatest advancements AI brings is the ability to generate full blocks of code from natural language descriptions.

How Developers Use Code Generation

You might type the following prompt:

> "Create a Python function that sorts a list of student records by grade, from highest to lowest, and returns the top five."

Within seconds, the AI returns a complete function with variable names, logic, and formatting.

What AI-Generated Code Is Good For

- Prototyping features quickly
- Trying different coding approaches
- Learning new languages by comparing examples
- Creating templates, services, APIs, and utilities

What Code Generation Does Not Replace

- Human architecture decisions
- Knowing the problem you are solving
- Understanding edge cases and performance
- Final responsibility for reviewing code for safety and correctness, even though AI can assist with automated checks

AI is fast, but only humans understand the real-world constraints of the system they are building.

Debugging—Finding and Fixing Bugs Faster

Debugging is one of the most time-consuming parts of software development. AI dramatically simplifies this by spotting issues that would take humans much longer to detect.

Where AI Helps

- Identifying logical errors in the code humans provide
- Spotting missing cases or incorrect assumptions
- Explaining error messages in plain English
- Suggesting fixes and detecting side effects
- Locating deeper systemic problems (e.g., poor data validation)

Why AI Is Effective at Debugging

AI models have been trained with millions of code samples, including common mistakes. This means they can often recognise patterns instantly, even across languages and frameworks.

A Practical Way to Use AI for Debugging

1. Paste the error message or failing test.
2. Include the relevant code block.
3. Ask: *"What is causing this issue, and how do I fix it?"*
4. Ask follow-up questions to confirm the fix is appropriate.

This guided, conversational debugging saves countless hours.

Documentation—Making Code Understandable

Documentation is essential but often neglected. AI finally makes documentation easy to create and maintain.

How AI Helps with Documentation

- Generate documentation comments automatically
- Write summaries of modules, classes, and functions
- Create usage examples and best practices
- Translate technical explanations into plain language
- Keep documentation consistent with the codebase

Vibe Coding: An Informal Term for Intent-Driven Development

In developer communities, this emerging development style is informally called *vibe coding*. It is not a formal methodology, but a shorthand for a way of working that has become more common with the rise of AI copilots and agents. The core idea is simple: the developer focuses on intent, direction, and problem framing, while AI assists with implementation details.

Instead of starting with exact syntax, work progresses through rapid iteration, feedback, and refinement. A developer describes what they want to achieve, reviews the AI-generated code, adjusts the direction, and iterates. The "vibe" refers to maintaining creative flow, with AI handling boilerplate, scaffolding, and repetitive tasks while the human concentrates on design decisions, logic, and trade-offs.

This style reflects how many developers already use modern AI tools. Used well, it can significantly speed up exploration and prototyping by reducing friction between ideas and implementation. It becomes easier to test concepts, try alternatives, and evolve a solution quickly.

However, vibe coding does **not** remove the need for engineering discipline. Code still needs to be reviewed, tested, secured, and understood by the person responsible for it. The AI may generate code, but accountability remains firmly with the developer.

Vibe coding is best understood as an informal working style enabled by AI, not a replacement for sound software practices. When combined with strong judgement and careful review, it can be a powerful way to work faster and more creatively without sacrificing quality or responsibility.

Mini Walkthrough — Building a Simple Feature With AI

This walkthrough demonstrates a small, realistic example: **creating a simple piece of logic to calculate late fees for a library system.**

Step 1: Describe the task

The task is described to the AI assistant in plain language, for example:

> "Create a small piece of logic, written in Java, that takes a due date and a return date, calculates how many days late a library book is, and applies a fee of R2.50 per day."

Step 2: AI generates the solution

The AI produces a clear solution that includes:

- handling dates
- calculating the number of late days
- computing the total fee

Step 3: Request improvements

Additional requirements are added, such as:

> "Include checks for invalid or reversed dates."

The AI updates the logic accordingly.

Step 4: Request documentation

Clear documentation is requested:

> "Add clear documentation comments explaining what this logic does, what inputs it expects, how the fee is calculated, and what

> the output represents. Use documentation style appropriate for the Java language."

The AI adds professional documentation automatically.

Step 5: Debug a failure

Testing reveals an issue with leap-year calculations. The problem is described.

> "Testing shows that the logic produces incorrect results for leap years. Please identify the issue in the date calculation, fix the leap-year handling, and explain what was changed."

The AI then corrects the logic and explains the change.

Step 6: Integrate into the codebase

To support usage and documentation, examples are requested:

> "Generate two example usages for the documentation."

This completes a simple but realistic workflow for developing, refining, and integrating a feature using AI assistance.

* * *

AI is reshaping software development—not by replacing programmers, but by amplifying their capabilities. Copilots reduce repetitive work, code generation speeds up development, debugging becomes collaborative, and documentation becomes almost effortless. These tools free developers to focus on design, judgement, creativity, and problem-solving—the human parts of software engineering.

In the next chapter, we expand from code into data: how AI assists with analysis, spreadsheets, automation, and everyday decision-making workflows. This is where technical and non-technical users alike begin to see how accessible these tools truly are.

23

AI for Data Analysis and Automation

Data analysis has traditionally been a skill associated with specialised training, formulas, and long hours spent cleaning and organising information. Modern AI tools change that. Today, anyone who works with data—whether in business, education, research, or personal projects—can use AI to clean datasets, generate formulas, understand patterns, and automate repeated tasks. What once required technical expertise can now be done through simple, natural-language instructions.

This chapter explores how AI supports data cleaning, spreadsheet analysis, formula generation, and workflow automation. It also includes practical mini projects you can try using sample or synthetic data, ensuring safe and responsible practice.

Data Cleaning

Data cleaning is often the most time-consuming part of data analysis. AI can dramatically reduce this effort by identifying and correcting inconsistencies.

Common Data-Cleaning Tasks AI Can Help With

- Removing duplicate entries
- Standardising date formats
- Correcting spelling inconsistencies
- Normalising capitalisation
- Identifying missing values
- Splitting or merging columns
- Extracting key information from longer text
- Converting unstructured text into clear categories

Sample prompt

> "Here is a sample list of customer names. Please remove duplicates, standardise the formatting, correct obvious spelling mistakes, and return a cleaned version."

Why Clean Data Matters

Clean data leads to:

- accurate calculations
- reliable formulas
- meaningful charts
- trustworthy analysis
- smoother automation

AI does not replace good data practices, but it drastically reduces manual labour.

Querying Spreadsheets

Spreadsheet tools like Excel or Google Sheets can be intimidating for newcomers, especially when formulas feel complex. AI allows users to explore data conversationally.

How Conversational Analysis Works

You describe the insight you want, and AI:

1. understands the structure of your table
2. performs the analysis
3. summarises the results
4. explains the steps if you would like to repeat them manually

Examples of Natural-Language Queries

- Which product had the highest sales this month?
- Group these entries by region and show the totals.
- Identify rows where the delivery time exceeded 14 days.
- Create an average-by-category summary table.

AI Can Be Asked to Explain Its Reasoning

Sample Prompt:

> "Please explain how you reached this result."

This makes data analysis accessible, even for people who rarely use spreadsheets.

Generating Formulas

AI is especially helpful when generating formulas—a task that can be confusing for beginners and tedious even for experienced users.

What AI Can Generate

- Excel formulas
- Google Sheets formulas
- SQL queries (for databases)
- Regular expressions for pattern matching
- Logical expressions for filtering or categorising

Sample Prompt:

> "Write a formula to extract the first name from a full name that contains multiple words."

The Value of AI-Generated Formulas

Users no longer need to memorise formula syntax or search for examples. AI provides the formula, an explanation, variations for different spreadsheet tools and suggestions for edge cases. This builds confidence and reduces errors.

Mini Projects—Practice Using Sample or Synthetic Data

To help you experience the workflow, here are three practical mini-projects using fictional data.

Mini Project 1: Cleaning a Sample Contact List

Goal: Practise cleaning a messy list of names, phone numbers, and email addresses using synthetic or dummy data.

Important Safety Reminder: never paste real customer details, personal information, or confidential records into a public AI tool.

Use:

- fictional names
- placeholder phone numbers
- invented email addresses
- synthetic datasets

Enterprises with secure AI systems may allow internal data use, but only under approved data policies.

Steps:

- Create a small fictional dataset with deliberate inconsistencies.
- Paste the synthetic data into an AI tool.
- Ask the AI to:
- remove duplicates
- standardise name formatting
- correct invalid email patterns
- format phone numbers consistently
- Request a clean, organised output.
- Ask for a summary of the changes made.

Outcome: A realistic data-cleaning experience carried out safely.

Mini Project 2: Analysing Sales Data Without Writing Formulas

Goal: Extract insights from a table containing fictional monthly sales data.

Steps:

– Create or copy a small synthetic dataset with product categories and sales figures.

– Ask the AI to:

– identify growth trends

– calculate averages

– highlight unusual values

– create a summary table

– Request formulas or steps for verification.

– Ask for charts or visual summaries if needed.

Outcome: A clear understanding of trends and averages without manually working through formulas.

Mini Project 3: Automating a Weekly Summary Task

Goal: Build a simple reporting process using synthetic performance data.

Steps:

– Describe the structure of your fictional dataset and the type of weekly summary you want.

– Ask the AI to:

– generate formulas

– create a template

– propose automation steps

– produce text summaries for a report

– Request instructions for repeating the process weekly.

> *Outcome:* A repeatable data workflow that reduces effort and demonstrates how AI can support ongoing reporting.

* * *

AI makes data analysis approachable for everyone. It simplifies everything from cleaning unstructured data to querying spreadsheets, generating formulas, and automating routine tasks. Instead of wrestling with syntax or endlessly searching for the right formula, users can focus on understanding what the data means and how it can support better decisions.

In the next chapter, we shift from spreadsheets to the foundations of modern AI systems themselves—APIs, embeddings, and vector search. These concepts sound technical, but with the clarity you have built so far, they will feel surprisingly intuitive.

24

APIs, Embeddings, Vector Search and Retrieval-Augmented Generation (RAG)

As AI becomes woven into everyday tools and products, certain building blocks appear repeatedly: APIs, embeddings, and vector search. These concepts often sound technical or intimidating, yet they are surprisingly intuitive once you understand their purpose. They form the practical infrastructure that allows AI systems to communicate with apps, understand meaning, and retrieve relevant information quickly and intelligently.

This chapter explains what each of these elements does, how they work together, and why they matter in real-world systems—from chatbots to recommendation engines to enterprise search tools.

What Are APIs

API stands for *Application Programming Interface*, but the name matters far less than the idea behind it. An API is simply a *bridge* that enables two systems talk to each other.

An Everyday Metaphor

Ordering food at a restaurant illustrates the concept well:

1. You tell the waiter what you want.
2. The waiter passes your request to the kitchen.
3. The kitchen handles the order behind the scenes.
4. The waiter brings it back.

The waiter is the API. You do not deal with the kitchen directly; you explain what you want, and the waiter handles the rest.

In Software

An API receives a request, sends it to another system and returns the result. You do not need to know how the other system works internally.

Why APIs Matter for AI

Many AI tools you use daily, chatbots, image generators, translation systems, and recommendation engines, are accessed via APIs. This enables websites, mobile apps, business software and automation tools to use powerful AI models without building them from scratch. For example, a developer can send the following message to an AI API:

> "Summarise this paragraph."

The AI returns a summary, and the application displays it. APIs are the practical glue that integrates AI into real products. ChatGPT, for example, is built on APIs: it sends your request to a model, receives the response, and presents it in a chat interface. Anyone can build similar applications by sending requests to these models through an API and displaying the results in their own interface.

Why Embeddings Matter

As discussed earlier, embeddings are numerical representations of meaning. They allow AI systems to recognise relationships between ideas—for example, the word *cat* is closer in meaning to *dog* than to *skyscraper.*

In real applications, embeddings do much more than store meaning. They drive features that depend on finding, comparing, or grouping information based on similarity, not just matching exact words.

Practical Uses of Embeddings

Embeddings enable AI systems to:

- Find relevant documents or messages by meaning, not just keywords
- Match questions to the most appropriate answers
- Classify text into themes or categories
- Group similar items together
- Detect duplicates or near-duplicates
- Personalise results based on user interests
- Retrieve relevant context for an AI assistant's next response

Why Embeddings Matter

Traditional systems rely on exact word matches. Embeddings enable AI to understand the *underlying meaning* behind words. This is what allows semantic search, recommendation engines, and AI assistants that can recall relevant information even when asked in different ways. Embeddings are the link between *raw text* and *meaningful retrieval.*

How Vector Databases Work

Once data is converted into embeddings, it becomes a list of numbers referred to as a **vector**. A vector database is designed specifically to store these vectors and find the most similar ones. Examples of vector databases include *Pinecone*, *Weaviate*, *Milvus*, *Qdrant*, and *ChromaDB*.

Why Traditional Databases Are Not Enough

Traditional databases—such as Oracle, MySQL, PostgreSQL, and SQL Server—work well for names, numbers, dates, and exact matches. Still, they are not designed to efficiently compare thousands of values to determine which items are most closely related in meaning.

What Vector Databases Do

Vector databases:

1. Store embeddings
2. Measure similarity between vectors
3. Return the closest matches

This enables systems to answer questions like:

- Which documents are most similar to this one?
- Which past customer issues are comparable to this one?
- Which products are most like the one just viewed?
- What information should the AI retrieve as context?

How Similarity Works

If two vectors are close together, their meanings are similar, and if they are far apart, the meanings differ. This mathematical relationship becomes a powerful tool for search, classification, memory, and recommendations.

Where Vector Databases Shine

Built to manage millions of items, support large-scale search, process real-time queries, and adapt to evolving datasets, vector databases form the engine that enables intelligent retrieval.

How Retrieval-Augmented Generation (RAG) Works

Large language models are powerful, but they have two major limitations: they cannot access your private documents, and they do not automatically know recent or domain-specific information. Retrieval-Augmented Generation (RAG) is a practical solution that provides an AI system access to the knowledge it needs, without changing the underlying model.

RAG works by combining two parts of the AI stack:

- a retrieval system that finds relevant information, and
- a language model that uses that information to generate an answer.

This enables the model to respond based on facts rather than guesses.

Why RAG Exists

RAG was created to solve real-world challenges that appear when using LLMs on their own:

- The model cannot "look up" answers in your documents.
- It may hallucinate on missing details.
- Its knowledge stops at the date it was trained.
- It cannot search through large collections of files.
- It should not be fine-tuned with private or sensitive data unless it runs in a secure, isolated enterprise environment.

RAG avoids these problems by retrieving the relevant information when needed, giving the model the exact context required to answer accurately.

When RAG Is Useful

RAG is ideal when your application needs:

- Answers based on internal or private documents
- Up-to-date information
- Accurate summaries of long reports
- Consistent responses without hallucinations
- A searchable knowledge base
- Enterprise-level control over what the model can and cannot access

RAG is used in customer support assistants, internal organisational chatbots, search tools, legal and policy-analysis systems, research environments, and enterprise AI platforms.

RAG vs Fine-Tuning

It is easy to confuse RAG with fine-tuning; however, they solve different problems.

- Fine-tuning adjusts the model's behaviour—its tone, style, or task-specific patterns.
- RAG supplements the model with information, facts, documents, and up-to-date knowledge.

Most production systems use RAG first because it is flexible, cost-effective, and does not alter the underlying model.

Why RAG Matters

RAG brings modern AI closer to how humans work. We do not memorise every detail—we retrieve information when we need it and apply reasoning on top. RAG allows AI systems to do the same, combining a knowledge lookup step with generative intelligence. This makes AI more reliable, grounded, and practical in real applications.

Real-World Examples—Where APIs, Embeddings, and Vector Search Come Together

These three tools rarely work independently. Most AI systems combine them into a pipeline:

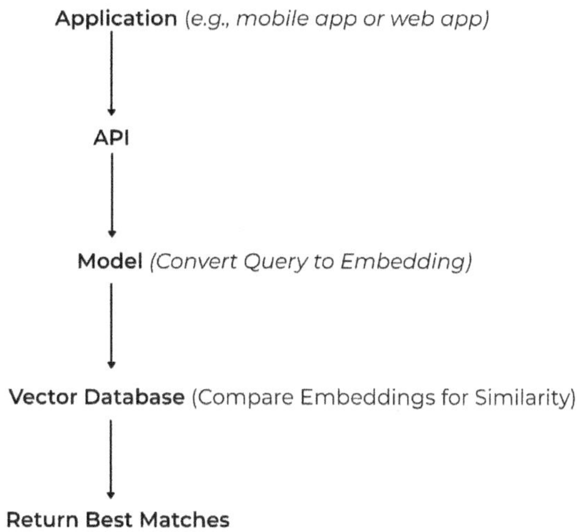

Figure 18.1: *How a query moves through the system—an application sends the request via an API, the model converts it to an embedding, the vector database performs a similarity search, and the best matches are returned.*

Here are some real examples.

1. Customer Support Chatbots

> *How it works:*
> – The user asks a question.
> – The question is converted into an embedding.
> – A vector database finds the most relevant help articles or past solutions.
> – An AI model uses the results to produce a helpful response.
>
> *Benefits:*
> – consistent answers
> – faster support
> – higher accuracy than keyword-based search

2. Recommendation Systems

> Streaming platforms, online shops, and social networks use embeddings to cluster similar items.
>
> *Process:*
> – Each item becomes an embedding
> – Similar embeddings are grouped
> – The system recommends the "closest neighbours"
>
> This improves discovery and personalisation.

AI Assistants with Memory

Some AI tools store key pieces of past conversations or user preferences as embeddings. When a new query arrives, the system retrieves relevant context using vector search, allowing responses that feel personalised and coherent.

Fraud Detection and Security

Embeddings can represent:

- transaction behaviour
- user activity patterns
- login sequences

Unusual behaviour appears as vectors that differ strongly from the norm, helping systems detect anomalies early.

Real-World Example: How an Internal Company Assistant Uses RAG

For example, in a company setting, an internal AI assistant can convert an employee's question into an embedding, search a vector database containing HR policies and internal documents, retrieve the most relevant passages, and then generate an answer grounded in the organisation's own knowledge.

> *User Query:* "What is our company's policy for working from home when a child is sick?"
>
> 1. The embedding model converts the query into a single embedding. This vector represents the meaning of the question.
>
> 2. The vector database searches company documents, and the system compares the query embedding with the embeddings of:
>   – HR policies
>   – employee handbook sections
>   – internal FAQs
>   – past HR announcements
>   – remote-work guidelines
>
> 3. The database then retrieves the most relevant passages, for example:
>   – "Remote Work Policy–Section 3: Family Care Situations"
>   – "Sick Leave and Dependent Care Guidelines (updated 2023)"
>
> 4. The retrieved documents are passed to the LLM, and the LLM receives the original question and the relevant policy excerpts. It does not guess, but bases its answer directly on the company documents.

5. The LLM generates a grounded answer

Sample response: "According to the Remote Work Policy – Section 3, employees may work from home when caring for a sick child, provided they notify their manager and can maintain core working hours. If the situation prevents normal productivity, dependent-care leave may be used. See the 2023 Dependent Care Guidelines for details."

The user receives an accurate response sourced from internal company data, with no hallucinations, outdated information, or exposure of private data. All the information comes from the organisation's own documents stored in the vector database.

The diagram below shows the same concept in a visual form:

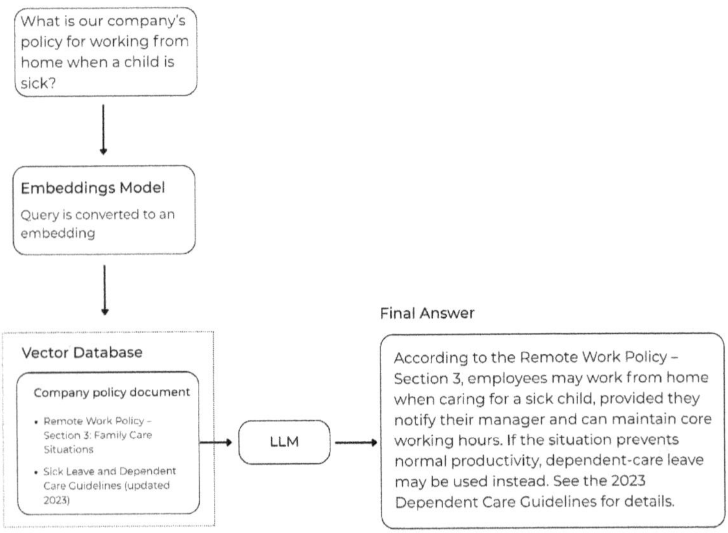

***Figure 18.2**: Retrieval-Augmented Generation in action. The system embeds the query, searches company documents for the closest matches, and the LLM produces an answer based on the retrieved information.*

Overview of How Document Chunks Are Loaded into a Vector Database

Before an AI system can retrieve relevant information, the company's documents must first be prepared and stored in a form that the vector database can search. The process begins by collecting the documents—such as policies, reports, or knowledge-base pages—and breaking them into smaller *chunks*.

Each chunk is then passed through an embedding model, which converts the text into a single numerical vector that captures its meaning. The vector database stores these vectors alongside the original chunk of text and useful metadata, such as the document name or section headings. Once this loading step is complete, the system can compare a user's query embedding to the stored vectors. If two texts have similar meaning, their embeddings will be close together, allowing the vector database to retrieve the most relevant chunks instantly.

Each entry stored in the vector database looks like this:

```
{
  "id": "remote_work_policy_003",
  "embedding": [
    -0.0142, 0.3281, -0.5527, 0.1194, 0.7743, -0.0038,
    -0.4479, 0.2156, 0.0892, -0.6321, 0.2547, 0.0193,
    ...
  ],
  "text": "Employees may work from home when caring for a sick
  child...",
  "metadata": {
    "document": "Remote Work Policy",
    "section": "Family Care",
    "page": 4
  }
}
```

* * *

APIs, embeddings, and vector search are the hidden infrastructure that make modern AI both powerful and practical. APIs allow systems to communicate. Embeddings provide AI a way to work with meaning. Vector databases enable rapid retrieval based on similarity. Understanding these concepts helps you appreciate how sophisticated AI features are built—and how they integrate seamlessly into everyday tools.

In the next chapter, we build on these foundations to explore *AI agents and automation workflows*—systems that use planning, reasoning, and tool-calling to complete tasks with minimal human prompting.

25

Agents and Automation Workflows

Up to this point, you have explored how AI understands information, generates language, retrieves knowledge, and integrates into applications. This chapter examines the next evolution of practical AI: systems that not only respond, but plan, act, and work on our behalf.

These emerging systems are known as AI agents. Agents represent one of the most exciting frontiers in AI, because they move beyond static answers and towards *dynamic, organised problem-solving.*

To understand them, we will explore what agents are, how they plan their actions, what frameworks they rely on, and what it means to design one conceptually—even if you have never built a system like this before.

What AI Agents Are

An AI agent is a system that:

1. Receives a goal or instruction
2. Breaks that goal into steps
3. Uses tools, APIs, or external systems to perform those steps
4. Observes the results

5. Adjusts its next action based on what it has learned

It behaves less like a calculator and more like a helpful digital assistant—one that works methodically, taking actions in sequence until the objective is achieved.

How Agents Differ from LLM Chat

A standard LLM answers questions, explains concepts, summarises text, and generates content, but operates within the scope of a single response.

An agent, by contrast, can browse the web, read documents, run code, call APIs, process results, and decide what to do next until a task is complete.

Agents have autonomy, not in making uncontrolled decisions, but in choosing the next best action towards a goal.

Simple Example

If you ask an LLM:

> "Find the three best flights to Cape Town under R3,000 and compare their refund policies."

A normal model will give a general explanation, but an agent will:

1. Search flight databases
2. Filter results
3. Extract refund policies
4. Summarise and compare
5. Deliver a final structured answer

It performs actual work, not just pattern-matching words.

ReAct, Tools, and Planning

Today's agents rely on several core ideas that allow them to think, act, and repeat. One of the most influential is *ReAct*, which stands for: *Reason + Act*

ReAct gives agents a structure for alternating between:

- *Reasoning*: thinking through what to do next
- *Acting*: using tools to gather information
- *Observing*: seeing what happened as a result
- *Continuing*: deciding on the next step

This loop continues until the task is complete.

What Are the Tools?

Tools are the building blocks that agents can use to perform real actions, such as:

- Accessing a database
- Running a code interpreter
- Fetching a URL
- Reading a PDF
- Querying a vector database
- Sending an email
- Writing to a spreadsheet

Tools transform an LLM from a static text generator into an active participant in a workflow.

Why Planning Matters

Because agents can act in the real world, planning is essential. A planning system helps the agent:

- understand the sequence of tasks
- avoid redundant steps
- correct mistakes
- optimise the workflow
- prevent risky actions

Planning frameworks ensure that agents are not simply reacting—they are progressing with structure and purpose.

Example: A simple ReAct loop for research

> *Goal*: Create a summary of the latest research on solar energy storage.
>
> The agent might reason:
> – "I should search for recent articles." -> Act: Web search
> – "I found three useful papers." -> Observe results
> – "I need to read each abstract." -> Act: Document reader
> – "Now I can summarise them together." -> Reason: Combine findings
> – "Task complete." -> Output final summary
>
> This loop is the beating heart of agent behaviour.

Workflow Orchestrations

A single agent can handle modest tasks in isolation, but more capable systems rely on multiple agents working together, each responsible for a part of the workflow. This is where workflow orchestration comes into play.

Orchestration acts as the coordinating layer, managing what each agent does, when actions occur, how information is shared, and how the overall workflow is structured.

Orchestration enables:

- multi-step pipelines
- parallel tasks
- quality checks
- fallback strategies
- error handling
- integration with business systems

Example: Automating a business report

> A well-orchestrated business report workflow might include:
> 1. *Data Agent* retrieves the latest sales numbers.
> 2. *Analysis Agent* cleans the data and identifies trends.
> 3. *Research Agent* checks industry benchmarks.
> 4. *Writing Agent* drafts the report.
> 5. *Review Agent* checks tone and clarity.
> 6. *Summary Agent* creates an executive overview.

Orchestration governs the order, dependencies, and flow of data between these steps.

Building a Conceptual Agent

Even without technical experience, you can understand the building blocks of designing an agent. At a high level, every agent has:

1. *A Goal:*
   What the agent is trying to accomplish.
   Example: "Prepare a weekly insights report."

2. *Inputs:*
   The information the agent receives at the beginning.
   Example: Data files, URLs, customer queries.

3. *Tools:*
   The actions the agent is allowed to perform.
   Example: "Search the web," "Query a database," "Run code."

4. *Reasoning Loop:*
   How the agent thinks, decides, and acts repeatedly until the task is complete.

5. *Memory or Working Context:*
   Short-term recall that helps the agent track progress.
   Example: Remembering the results of earlier steps.

6. *Constraints:*
   Boundaries that keep the system safe.
   Example: "Never send external emails without approval."

7. *Final Output:*
   The completed result.

> *Example:* A formatted report, a set of recommendations, a completed analysis.

Example: Designing a Customer-Support Agent

> *Goal*: Handle common product questions accurately using internal documents.
>
> *Tools*:
> - Read from the company's vector database
> - Retrieve FAQs
> - Summarise responses
> - Provide troubleshooting steps
>
> *Agent Workflow*:
> 1. Understand the customer question.
> 2. Convert it into an embedding.
> 3. Retrieve relevant documents.
> 4. Extract the necessary information.
> 5. Generate a clear, helpful response.
> 6. Ask if the customer needs anything else

Although it is simple, this agent saves hours of support time each week and improves customer experience.

The Promise of Agents

Agents mark a profound shift in how we work with AI. Instead of merely using tools, we increasingly collaborate with systems that perform real work—from research and automation to creative production.

They help automate repetitive tasks, explore ideas more deeply, coordinate complex processes, improve decision-making, and free humans to focus on work that requires judgement.

The future of agents is not about replacing people; it is about expanding human capability by giving us intelligent partners that work alongside us.

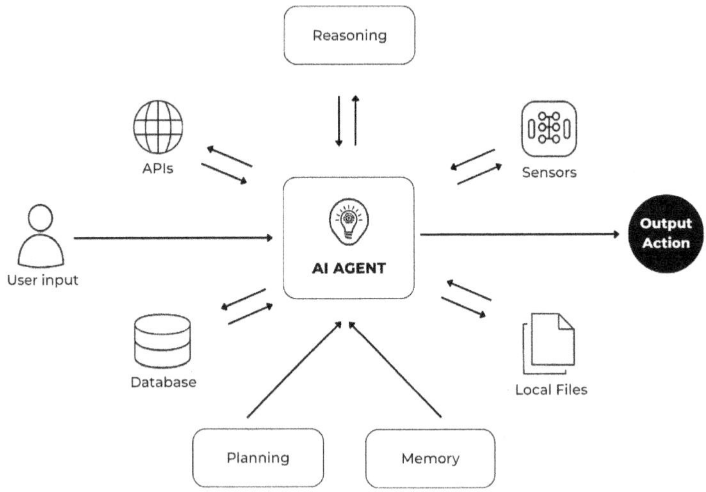

***Figure 19.1**: A high-level view of an AI agent interacting with user input, external systems, and its own reasoning, planning, and memory processes. In practice, agents access external systems through controlled tools, but conceptually, it is sufficient to view the agent retrieving information directly from databases, APIs, files, and sensors.*

* * *

Agents move AI from static responses to dynamic action. They utilise reasoning loops such as ReAct, integrate with real-world tools, and operate inside orchestrated workflows. With the right design, an agent can analyse data, retrieve documents, coordinate tasks, and produce meaningful results—all with minimal human intervention.

In the next chapter, we explore how non-technical creators can build powerful AI systems using *no-code platforms*, opening the door for anyone to design intelligent workflows without writing a single line of code.

26

Building AI Projects Without Coding

For most of computing history, building software required writing code. If you did not know how to program, you could not turn an idea into a working system. That boundary has now shifted. Modern no-code platforms enable the designing of AI-powered tools, automate workflows, and even create full applications—all without touching a programming language. You focus on the logic. The platform handles the engineering.

This chapter introduces the no-code landscape, shows when it is the right choice, explains how to think like a systems designer even without technical skills, and guides you through building a small AI project.

Understanding No-Code Platforms

No-code platforms offer visual environments where you create software by connecting blocks, configuring settings, dragging components onto a screen, or linking steps in a workflow. Instead of writing instructions in a programming language, you assemble them through user-friendly interfaces.

Various platforms specialise in different tasks. Some are designed for automation—connecting services so that when an event triggers in one place, an action occurs in another. Others allow you to build full applications with screens, forms, data tables, and AI features. Many platforms now include built-in AI integrations, allowing the addition of an AI step through simple configuration, much like adding a form or connecting to a database.

The significance of these platforms is profound: they turn AI development from a specialist skill into something accessible to small businesses, educators, entrepreneurs, or anyone with a problem to solve.

No-Code, Low-Code, and Full-Code: The Difference

These terms describe a spectrum of how software is built, from visual configuration to complete programming control.

No-code platforms enable users to build applications through visual interfaces and configuration, rather than programming. Logic is created by connecting components, setting rules, and defining workflows. No-code is ideal for prototypes, internal tools, automation, and straightforward applications where speed and accessibility are most important.

Low-code platforms sit in the middle. They provide visual building blocks, such as no-code tools, but also allow developers to insert custom code when needed. This approach is useful when most of the application can be assembled visually, but certain features require deeper customisation or optimisation.

Full-code development involves writing software entirely through programming languages and frameworks. It offers the greatest flexibility and control, making it suitable for complex, large-scale, or performance-critical systems. However, it also requires specialised skills and significantly more development time.

Rather than competing approaches, these models complement one another. Many projects begin with no-code to explore ideas quickly, evolve into low-code as requirements grow, and eventually move to full-code when complexity demands it.

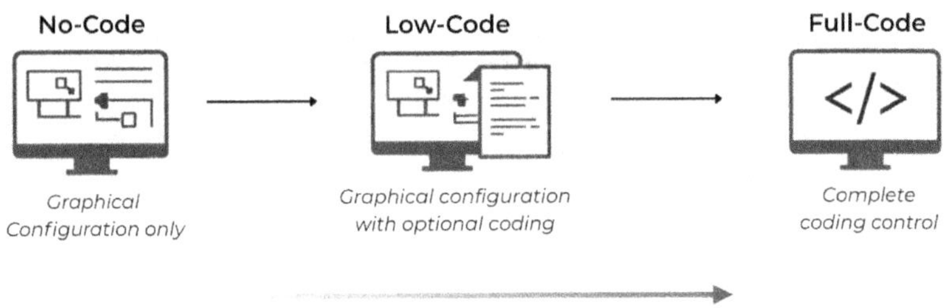

***Figure 20.1**: No-code, low-code, and full-code development as a spectrum of increasing flexibility and control.*

No-Code Is Enough When:

- The workflow is predictable and structured
- The data sources are simple (spreadsheets, forms, basic APIs)
- You are building a prototype or internal tool
- You need to automate repetitive tasks
- The number of users is small or moderate
- You are exploring ideas and experimenting

Typical examples:

- A customer-support assistant pulling answers from company documents
- A content-generation assistant
- A dashboard that summarises weekly reports
- An AI-powered form that checks input quality

- A personal productivity app

No-code solutions thrive where logic is clear and complexity is limited.

No-Code May Not Be Enough When:

- You need custom logic that no platform supports
- You require fast performance at scale
- You must integrate deeply with corporate systems
- Your application needs strict security or advanced user control
- You are building a production product for thousands of users
- You need full RAG pipelines with custom embeddings and database tuning

In these cases, low-code or full-code solutions eventually become necessary.

A helpful rule of thumb:

> *Start with no-code to validate the concept. Move to full code only when the problem outgrows the platform.*

This saves enormous time and cost.

Applying Systems Thinking Without Writing Code

Even in a no-code environment, you are still designing a system—something that responds to an input, performs a process, and produces an output. Thinking in terms of systems makes building AI workflows much easier.

Start by identifying what triggers the workflow. It might be a form submission, a message in a chat interface, the arrival of a file, or a scheduled event. Once you know what starts the process, consider what the AI is meant to do: summarise information, analyse content, extract details, draft a response, or make a recommendation.

AI rarely acts alone. Additional steps may be necessary before or after the result produced by the AI, such as cleaning data, reading documents, looking up information, validating results, or routing information to another system. These surrounding steps give shape to the overall workflow.

Finally, decide what should happen once the AI generates its answer. Will the output appear in a chat? Should it be emailed to someone, saved in a database, or posted to a dashboard? Clarifying this early makes the entire project easier to design.

Systems thinking also includes boundaries. Even no-code developers must consider what data should never be sent to an AI model, whether certain actions require confirmation, and how the system should behave if the AI is uncertain. These safeguards turn a workflow into something reliable and responsible.

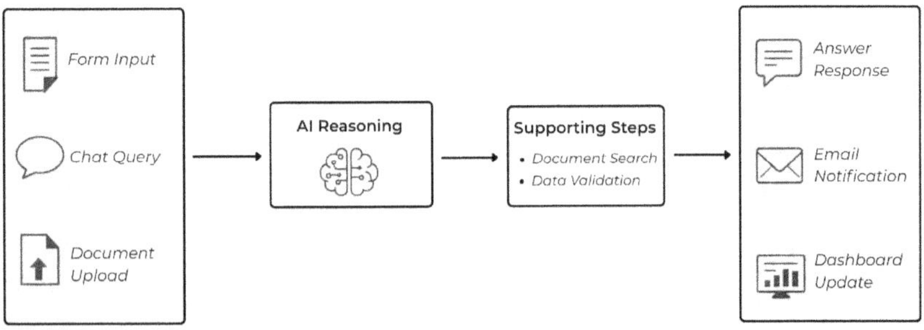

***Figure 20.2**: Systems thinking applied to a no-code AI workflow, showing how inputs flow through AI decision-making and supporting steps to produce meaningful outputs.*

A Guided No-Code Project: Build a Document-Answering Assistant

To make these ideas concrete, let us create a simple AI project that answers questions based on documents you provide. You will not write any code; the goal is to understand the flow behind an AI-enabled tool.

This type of document-based AI assistant can be built using no-code tools such as OpenAI custom GPTs, Voiceflow, Zapier, or application builders like Bubble, each offering different levels of control and flexibility.

Begin by gathering a few sample documents such as public guides, product descriptions, or FAQ pages. Avoid uploading private or sensitive material unless the platform explicitly guarantees strict data isolation and access controls. Most no-code tools will either allow you to paste the text directly or upload the files for the system to process.

Next, create a way for users to submit questions. This might be a text field, a chat interface, or a form. Whatever the method, this input will trigger the workflow.

When the question is received, the system sends it to the AI model for processing. Many platforms provide an "AI" or "LLM" action. Ask the model to interpret the question and prepare for retrieval. Some tools include built-in document search, while others may require you to configure a basic lookup or keyword match behind the scenes.

Once you retrieve relevant text, feed both the question and the retrieved material back to the AI with clear instructions to answer only using the provided information. This helps reduce hallucinations and ensures grounded responses.

Finally, choose how to present the answer: display it to the user, send it via email, record it in a table, or trigger the next step in your workflow. You have now created a real, functioning AI tool using only no-code features.

You can extend this project indefinitely by allowing follow-up questions, storing past queries, adding more documents, or notifying a human when certain topics appear. No-code development accelerates experimentation, letting you focus on the outcome rather than the infrastructure.

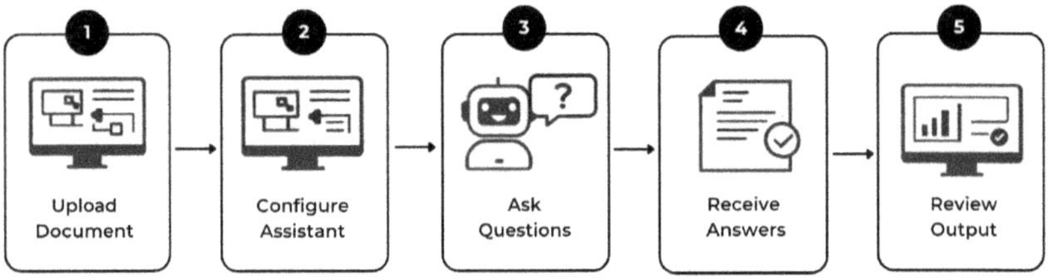

Figure 20.3: *A guided no-code workflow for building a document-answering assistant, showing how documents are uploaded, the assistant is configured, questions are asked, answers are generated, and results are reviewed with human oversight.*

The Power of Building Without Code

The rise of no-code AI is not about lowering quality—it is about widening participation. By removing the barrier of programming expertise, no-code gives creators, teachers, analysts, founders, and everyday users the ability to build tools that once required full engineering teams.

What matters most is not writing code. It is understanding the problem, imagining the solution, and designing the flow. Once you develop systems thinking, no-code platforms can turn those ideas into working solutions with minimal friction.

Your creativity becomes the engine; the platform becomes the instrument. And with AI integrated directly into these tools, the range of what you can build is expanding faster than ever.

V

PART 5—Minds and Machines: The Deep, Future-Oriented Section

Part 5 looks beyond today and explores how AI will shape our work, thinking, and future. Here, we step back from the mechanics and consider the bigger questions—what changes are coming, how we can prepare, and what it means to live in a world where minds and machines coexist. It is a hopeful, forward-looking guide to the road ahead.

27

A Short Story: The Choice That Remained Human

Chipo stood at the window long after the office lights had dimmed.

Below, the city moved with a rhythm she recognised—people heading home, screens glowing, systems humming quietly in the background. Much of that motion, she knew, was now shaped by algorithms: schedules optimised, traffic adjusted, decisions subtly nudged.

None of it felt dramatic, and yet, everything felt different.

Earlier that day, she had watched a presentation about the future of work. Some roles would change. Others would disappear. New ones would emerge. The technology itself was impressive, but what lingered was not capability—it was pace.

The changes were no longer hypothetical.

She thought about how her own work had shifted. AI now supports tasks that once demanded intense focus. Ideas formed faster. Learning happened on demand. AI did not replace her thinking, but it quietly reshaped it—how she explored problems, how she reflected, how she decided what mattered.

That unsettled her slightly.

Was this still her thinking—or something shared? The question followed her home.

Later that evening, she read an article debating whether machines could ever become conscious. Some argued it was inevitable. Others insisted intelligence and consciousness were fundamentally different. Chipo was not certain where she stood, but she sensed the distinction mattered more than most people realised.

If machines could act intelligently without awareness, responsibility could never belong to them; it had to remain human.

That thought led her deeper into ethics, rules, and shared expectations. Every powerful technology had forced society to renegotiate its boundaries, and AI was no exception—except this time, the technology participated directly in decisions that affected lives.

Who set the limits? Who remained accountable? And how did society prepare people—not just systems—for what came next?

Chipo realised then that the future was not something AI would deliver on its own. It would be shaped by choice: how people designed systems, governed their use, trained for change, and protected what mattered most—by whether they treated AI as a force to surrender to, or a tool to steward with care.

What she felt was not fear, but resolve.

The road ahead was not fixed. It was not written into code or locked inside models. It was still open.

And in a world of increasingly intelligent machines, the most important work remained deeply human.

> *This fictional story introduces the themes of* ***Part 5***.

28

The Future of Work in The Age of AI

Every major technological shift reshapes how people work. The printing press transformed access to literacy, shifting reading and writing from an elite skill to a widespread human capability. Electricity transformed factories and cities. Computers reshaped offices, communication, and entire industries. Artificial Intelligence is the next shift on this scale, not because it replaces effort, but because it redefines where human effort matters most.

The future of work is not a simple story of jobs disappearing or machines taking over. It is a story of roles evolving, new forms of work emerging, and skills being redefined. Understanding this shift helps reduce fear and foster a sense of readiness.

This chapter explores how work is changing, where new opportunities are arising, and how individuals can stay relevant as intelligent systems become integrated into daily work life.

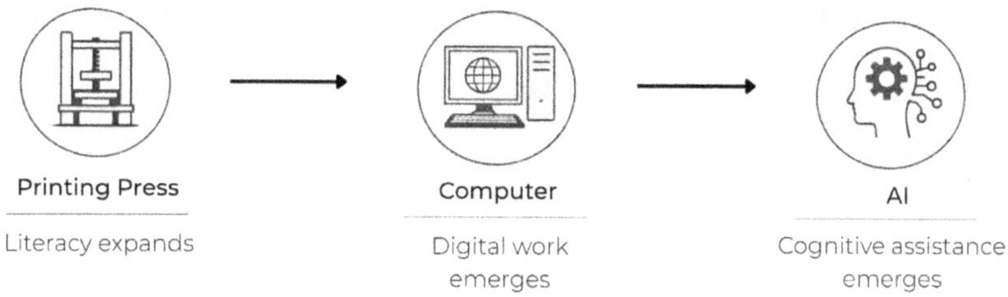

Figure 21.2: *Major technology shifts and how they reshaped human work—literacy expanded with the printing press, digital work emerged with computers, and cognitive assistance emerged with AI.*

How Jobs Are Changing

AI does not replace jobs entirely; it reshapes them from within. While demand for certain roles may decline, AI more often reshapes jobs by changing the tasks they involve rather than eliminating them outright.

Most roles have a mix of repetitive, creative, social, and strategic tasks. AI excels at recognising patterns, handling repetition, summarising information, and making predictions. As these capabilities are woven into everyday work, roles evolve from the inside rather than disappearing altogether.

For example:

- Accountants spend less time on data entry and more time on interpretation and advisory work.
- Software developers spend less time writing routine, repetitive code and more time focusing on system design and clearly defining the problems they are solving.
- Marketers automate content drafting and analytics while focusing on strategy, storytelling, and audience insight.

- Customer service agents rely on AI for rapid responses, background information, and guidance while handling complex or emotionally sensitive interactions.

In each case, the role does not vanish; instead, the centre of gravity shifts toward judgement, context, and decision-making.

The most significant change is not the loss of work, but the reduction of *purely mechanical effort.* Work becomes less about executing steps and more about guiding systems, validating outcomes, and making informed choices.

Jobs That Are Emerging

As old tasks fade into the background, new roles are forming—many of which did not exist just a few years ago.

Some of these roles sit close to the technology:

- AI product managers who define how AI features should behave.
- Prompt designers and workflow architects who shape how humans interact with models.
- AI operations specialists who monitor performance, safety, and reliability.
- Data curators who prepare, organise, and govern information used by AI systems.

Others are more human-centred:

- Ethics and governance professionals focused on fairness, accountability, and responsible use.
- Educators and trainers who adapt learning experiences for AI-augmented environments.
- Domain experts who combine subject knowledge with AI tools to increase

impact.

Many future roles will not include the word "AI" in their titles. Instead, AI will only be part of how the job is done, much like email, spreadsheets, or search engines today.

> *The most valuable people will be those who understand both the problem space and how to collaborate with intelligent tools.*

Staying Relevant in an AI-Driven World

Staying relevant does not require becoming a machine-learning engineer or mastering every new tool. It requires developing *adaptability*.

In the age of AI, relevance comes from:

- Understanding what AI can and cannot do.
- Knowing how to ask better questions, not just get faster answers.
- Being able to evaluate outputs rather than accepting them blindly.
- Applying human judgement where context, values, or consequences matter.

People who struggle are often those who treat AI as a replacement for thinking. People who thrive treat it as a thinking partner.

Relevance also comes from curiosity. The tools will continue to change, but the habit of learning—experimenting, reflecting, and adjusting—remains timeless.

AI rewards those willing to evolve with it, not those who resist or defer entirely to it.

Skill Evolution

As AI takes over more mechanical or repetitive tasks, certain human skills become more important rather than decline.

These include:

- *Critical thinking:* evaluating outputs, spotting errors, and questioning assumptions.
- *Systems thinking:* understanding how parts interact within larger processes.
- *Communication:* explaining ideas clearly to both humans and machines.
- *Creativity:* generating new perspectives, not just variations of the old.
- *Ethical reasoning:* considering impact, bias, and responsibility.
- *Emotional intelligence:* navigating collaboration, leadership, and trust.

Technical skills still matter, but they become outdated more quickly. Conceptual skills endure longer. While technical skills focus on *how* to do something, conceptual skills focus on *what* should be done and *why*.

The future belongs to people who can move fluidly between thinking, deciding, and guiding intelligent systems—rather than competing with them at speed or scale.

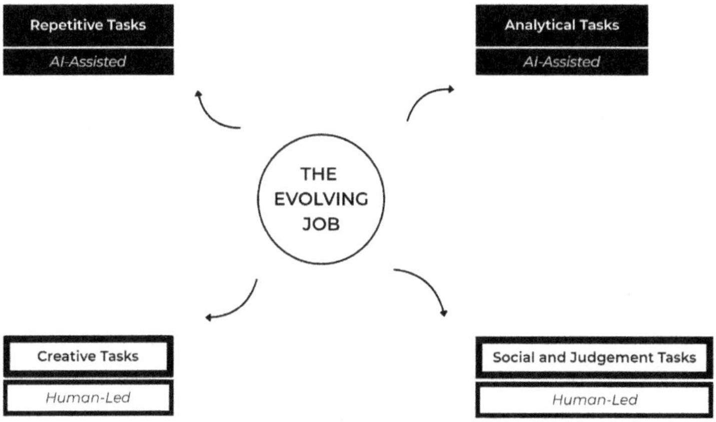

***Figure 21.1**: Jobs evolve as tasks are redistributed—AI assists repetitive and analytical work, while humans remain central to creative, social, and judgement-based tasks.*

Work as Partnership, Not Competition

One of the most important mindset shifts is to view AI as a collaborator rather than a replacement in the workplace.

AI has no goals, no values, and no accountability of its own. It also does not understand the meaning or the consequences. Those responsibilities continue to rest with humans. The most successful workplaces of the future will be those that design collaboration thoughtfully:

- Clearly defined boundaries for what should and should not be automated.
- Human oversight in high-stakes or consequential decisions.
- Transparency in how AI-supported decisions are generated and used.
- Continuous learning woven into everyday work practices.

In this model, AI amplifies human capability rather than diminishing it.

* * *

The future of work in the age of AI is not predetermined. It will be shaped by choices—how organisations deploy tools, how individuals adapt, and how societies define responsibility and value.

Jobs will change. New ones will emerge. Skills will evolve, but human relevance does not disappear; it shifts upwards, towards meaning, judgement, and stewardship.

Those who embrace AI as a partner, remain curious, and continue to grow will not be replaced by machines. They will help define what meaningful work looks like in an intelligent world.

In the next chapter, we step even deeper—beyond work itself—to explore how AI challenges our ideas of intelligence, creativity, and what it means to be human.

29

How AI Changes Human Thinking

AI not only changes what we do, but also how we think.

Throughout history, tools have shaped human cognition. Writing reduced the need to memorise long stories. Calculators changed how people approach arithmetic. Search engines altered how information is recalled. AI represents the next step in this lineage, not by replacing human thinking, but by reshaping how mental effort is applied.

This chapter examines how AI influences human thinking, reshapes reasoning habits, and why this matters in a world of intelligent systems that increasingly act as thinking partners.

Cognitive Offloading

Cognitive offloading refers to the practice of shifting mental tasks to external systems, such as software, devices, or AI-based assistants. Humans do this constantly: calendars remember dates, maps handle navigation, and notebooks store ideas. AI expands this dramatically.

With AI, people can offload:

- Drafting and rewriting text
- Summarising complex material
- Organising ideas
- Exploring multiple possibilities quickly
- Holding large amounts of contextual information

This offloading is not inherently negative. In many cases, it frees mental capacity for higher-level thinking such as judgement, creativity, and strategic decision-making.

However, there is a subtle trade-off. When cognitive effort is reduced too far, skills can atrophy. Over-reliance on AI for explanation, synthesis, or reasoning can weaken the very abilities AI is meant to support.

Cognitive offloading has always existed; what matters now is how deliberately it is applied. AI is most powerful when it handles routine cognitive load while humans retain responsibility for meaning, direction, and evaluation.

The Extended Mind

The concept of the *extended mind* suggests that human cognition extends beyond the brain. Tools, notes, diagrams, and now AI systems become part of the thinking process itself.

When a person thinks through a problem by conversing with an AI tool, explores ideas through iterative prompts, and refines understanding through feedback, it moves beyond a tool and becomes a cognitive partner.

This does not mean the AI understands or thinks; it means humans increasingly think with AI, not merely through it. The boundary between human reasoning that happens in the mind and external assistance from tools becomes increasingly blurred.

Used well, AI can deepen insight. Used poorly, it can reduce original thought. The difference lies in whether AI is treated as:

- A *crutch*, replacing thinking
- Or a *scaffold*, supporting it

The future of effective thinking belongs to those who integrate AI into their cognitive process without surrendering decision-making to the machine.

Example: When Humans Hand Decision-Making Over to Machines

> A well-known incident involved a lawyer who used an AI system for legal research. The AI confidently generated case references that appeared legitimate, complete with citations and summaries. However, the cases did not exist.
>
> The lawyer submitted the material to the court without verifying the sources. When the court attempted to locate the cited cases, it became clear that they were fabricated. The responsibility did not lie with the AI system, which was doing what it was designed to do—generate plausible text—but with the human professional who failed to validate the output.
>
> This case illustrates what happens when human judgement is deferred to a machine. The lawyer did not use AI as a research aid; instead, judgement and verification were implicitly delegated to the system. In high-stakes contexts such as law, medicine, or finance, this loss of human oversight can have serious consequences.
>
> The lesson is not that AI should be avoided, but that human responsibility does not transfer to the machine. AI can assist with

> exploration and drafting, but accountability for truth, accuracy, and consequences remains with us, humans.

How Humans Reason and How AI Produces Answers

Humans and AI reason in fundamentally different ways.

Human reasoning is:

- Contextual and experiential
- Influenced by emotion and intuition
- Capable of moral judgement
- Shaped by goals and values

AI reasoning is:

- Statistical and pattern-based
- Detached from lived experience
- Unaware of consequences
- Optimised for probability, not meaning

An AI does not understand an idea the way a human does. It predicts what comes next based on learned patterns. This makes AI remarkably effective at synthesis, analogy, and explanation, but unreliable when truth, intent, or responsibility are crucial.

This difference helps explain why AI can sound confident yet be incorrect, insightful yet miss nuance, or helpful yet lack wisdom.

Human thinking remains essential where:

- Trade-offs must be evaluated

- Ambiguity must be tolerated
- Ethical judgement is required
- Long-term consequences matter

The most effective thinkers of the AI era will be those who understand what kind of reasoning they are delegating, and what must remain human.

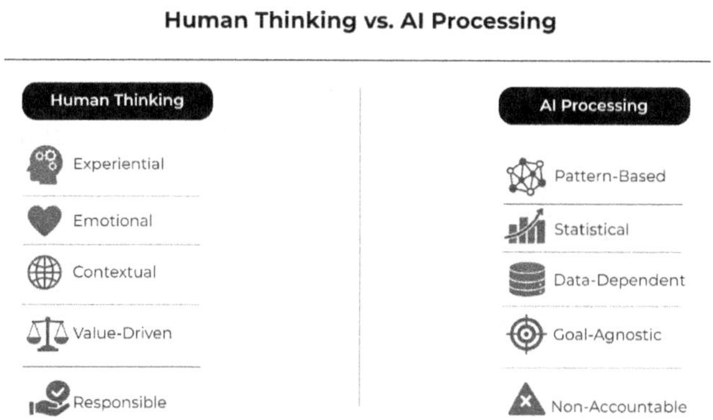

***Figure* 22.1**: *A comparison between human thinking and AI processing, highlighting how human reasoning is experiential, value-driven, and accountable, while AI operates through pattern-based, statistical processing without understanding, intent, or responsibility.*

Human Bias vs. Model Bias

Bias exists in both humans and AI, but it takes different forms.

Human bias often arises from:

- Personal experience
- Cultural background
- Emotional reactions

- Social identity and incentives

Model bias arises from:

- Training data imbalances
- Historical patterns encoded in text
- Overrepresentation of dominant perspectives
- Statistical averaging of human viewpoints

AI does not invent bias; it *reflects and amplifies* patterns present in the data it learns from. This can make bias appear more neutral or authoritative than it truly is. Unlike humans, AI cannot recognise or correct its own bias. It does not question assumptions or reflect on fairness. That responsibility remains with the human user. Understanding this distinction is critical. AI outputs should not be treated as objective truth, but as probabilistic reflections of human-generated data.

Human judgement is required to detect missing perspectives, challenge default assumptions, and interpret results within real-world contexts.

AI can assist thinking, but it cannot replace ethical awareness.

Thinking Well in the Age of AI

AI is not diminishing human thinking; it is *reconfiguring it.*

The challenge of the AI era is not learning to use tools, but learning how to think *alongside* them. This requires:

- Awareness of cognitive offloading
- Intentional use of AI as a thinking partner
- Clear boundaries between assistance and authority
- Continuous reflection on bias and judgement

Those who develop these skills will not lose their capacity for deep thinking. They will think differently, more expansively, and more strategically.

As AI becomes part of everyday thinking, the future belongs to those who remain curious, reflective, and intentional about how their minds develop in partnership with intelligent tools.

30

Consciousness and Intelligence

The question of whether machines can be conscious remains one of the most debated topics in AI. We are comfortable talking about machines that calculate, predict, and generate language. But we are less certain when we begin asking whether they *understand*, *experience*, or *feel*. This chapter clarifies the distinction between intelligence and consciousness, and explains why it is important to separate scientific understanding from speculation.

Understanding this boundary is essential—not only for technical accuracy, but for preserving clarity about what machines are and what humans uniquely remain.

Understanding Intelligence

At its core, intelligence refers to the ability to solve problems, adapt to new situations, learn from experience, and apply knowledge to achieve goals. By this definition, AI systems are undeniably intelligent in a functional sense. They can recognise patterns in vast datasets, optimise decisions, translate languages, and outperform humans in narrow domains. However, intelligence does not require awareness.

A calculator is intelligent in its ability to perform arithmetic flawlessly.

A navigation system intelligently finds the shortest route. An AI model intelligently predicts the next word in a sentence. None of these systems is aware of the tasks they perform. Human intelligence, by contrast, is inseparable from lived experience. It is shaped by emotion, memory, embodiment, social context, and subjective meaning. Humans do not merely solve problems; they care about outcomes, reflect on consequences, and assign value to their actions.

This distinction matters because much of the public conversation confuses *capability* and *consciousness*. A system that produces convincing language or creative output may appear human-like, but appearance alone is not evidence of inner experience.

> *High intelligence does not imply awareness.*
> *Performance is not experience.*

Could Machines Ever Be Conscious?

Consciousness is notoriously difficult to define, even among neuroscientists and philosophers. At a minimum, it involves subjective experience—the feeling of being aware, of having thoughts, sensations, and a sense of self. Current AI systems do not possess this. They do not experience curiosity, confusion, pain, or understanding. They have no desires, intentions, or self-awareness. When an AI says "I think" or "I understand," it is using language patterns learned from human text, not reporting an internal mental state.

The open question is whether consciousness could ever emerge in machines. Some researchers argue that consciousness might arise if systems become sufficiently complex or integrated. Others maintain that consciousness requires biological processes, embodiment, or evolutionary pressures that machines fundamentally lack. It is also possible that consciousness cannot be engineered at all, but emerges only under conditions we do not yet understand.

At present, no AI system meets even the weakest scientific criteria for consciousness. Claims that today's models are sentient or self-aware are not supported by evidence. Importantly, uncertainty about the future does not justify confusion in the present. Responsible speculation requires grounding discussion in what systems actually do rather than what their outputs resemble.

Science vs. Speculation

Science advances through testable hypotheses, empirical evidence, and cautious interpretation. Speculation, while valuable for imagination and long-term thinking, becomes misleading when it is presented as fact.

Much of the public anxiety about AI consciousness stems from anthropomorphism—the human tendency to project emotions, intentions, and inner life onto anything that behaves in familiar ways. Language models are especially prone to triggering this effect because language is our primary signal of the mind.

Fluent speech is not proof of awareness. An AI model does not reflect on its answers. Neither does it know if it is correct. It does not experience doubt or insight; it produces responses by statistically relating symbols based on prior data, guided by objectives defined by humans.

Recognising this helps shift the conversation towards more productive questions:

- How should intelligent systems be designed and governed?
- Where must human judgement remain central?
- What responsibilities do humans carry when deploying powerful tools?

These are ethical and societal challenges—not metaphysical ones.

Intelligence vs. Consciousness

Confusing intelligence with consciousness risks two serious mistakes.:

- *over-trust*—delegating decisions, judgement, or responsibility to systems that cannot understand consequences or moral weight.
- *misplaced fear*—treating tools as existential threats rather than systems shaped by human choices, incentives, and oversight.

Understanding what AI is *not* helps clarify what humans uniquely are. Humans remain the only agents capable of meaning, values, responsibility, and care. Machines can extend cognition, amplify capability, and support decision-making—but they do not replace moral agency. The future will not be defined by whether machines become conscious; it will be shaped by how deliberately humans choose to design, use, and govern intelligent systems.

* * *

Artificial intelligence challenges us not by thinking like humans, but by performing intellectual tasks without understanding them. Intelligence and consciousness are not the same, and treating them as such obscures both science and ethics.

As AI systems grow more capable, clarity becomes more important than speculation. The real question is not whether machines will become conscious, but whether humans will remain attentive to their responsibilities when using them.

In the final chapter of this book, we turn inwards—exploring what it means to remain human in an age of intelligent machines, and how values, purpose, and wisdom shape the future far more than algorithms ever will.

31

Ethics, Regulation and The Social Contract

As artificial intelligence becomes embedded in daily life, a deeper question emerges—one that goes beyond performance, productivity, or innovation.

Who Is Responsible for AI's Actions?

AI does not exist in isolation. It shapes decisions, influences behaviour, and increasingly participates in systems that affect people's livelihoods, safety, and rights. As its capabilities expand, so too must our frameworks for accountability, governance, and ethical responsibility. This chapter examines how societies are beginning to respond and explains why the conversation ultimately points to a new social contract between humans and the technologies they create.

Accountability in An Age of Intelligent Systems

Accountability has always been central to functioning societies. When actions cause harm or produce consequences, responsibility must lie somewhere. With AI, this principle becomes harder—but more important—than ever.

AI systems do not possess intent, values, or moral judgement. They cannot be praised, blamed, or punished. Therefore, responsibility cannot belong to the machine; it must remain with humans: designers, developers, organisations, and institutions that deploy these systems.

Yet AI complicates accountability in subtle ways. Decisions may be influenced by complex models, vast datasets, or automated processes that are difficult to *audit* or *explain*. When an outcome is undesirable, it can be tempting to say "the system decided" rather than examining the human choices embedded in its design and use.

Ethical AI demands resisting that temptation. Clear accountability requires transparency about how systems are built, tested, deployed, and monitored. It also requires recognising that responsibility does not disappear when decision-making becomes automated—it merely shifts upstream.

In the future of work and governance, accountability will increasingly mean owning not just outcomes, but the decision to delegate judgement to a machine in the first place.

Global Regulation

Around the world, governments and institutions are racing to keep pace with rapid technological change. Unlike earlier technologies, AI does not respect borders. Models trained in one country may be deployed globally, influencing millions of people across different legal, cultural, and ethical contexts. As a result, regulation is emerging unevenly.

Some regions adopt risk-based approaches and impose stricter requirements on AI systems used in sensitive areas such as healthcare, finance, hiring, or law enforcement. Others emphasise innovation and voluntary guidelines, wary of stifling progress through overly rigid rules.

Despite these differences, common themes are beginning to emerge:

- Transparency about how AI systems operate
- Human oversight for high-impact decisions
- Protection of individual rights and privacy
- Mechanisms for redress when harm occurs

Regulation, however, is not simply about control. At its best, it provides clarity—setting boundaries that enable trust, adoption, and long-term innovation. The challenge lies in crafting rules that are flexible enough to adapt, and yet firm enough to protect human interests.

AI governance is still evolving and will likely be an ongoing process rather than a fixed framework.

Safety Challenges in Complex Systems

AI safety involves not only preventing dramatic failures but also managing subtle risks that emerge as systems interact with people, data, and institutions over time.

Some risks are technical: models may behave unpredictably outside their training conditions, amplify hidden biases, or produce outputs that appear confident but are incorrect. Other risks are social, such as over-reliance on automation, erosion of human judgement, or unequal impacts across different groups.

There is also the challenge of scale. An error made by a human affects a limited context. An error made by a widely deployed AI system can propagate instantly and broadly.

Addressing these challenges requires a shift in mindset. Safety cannot be treated as a one-time checklist. It must be an ongoing process involving monitoring, feedback, updates, and—critically—the willingness to pause or withdraw systems when risks outweigh benefits. In this sense, AI safety is less about flawless systems and more about responsible stewardship.

Like any system connected to networks, data, or software infrastructure, AI systems are exposed to security threats. Malicious actors may exploit vulnerabilities, manipulate inputs, poison training data, or misuse automated systems for harmful purposes. These risks arise not because AI is intelligent, but because it operates within complex technical environments that can be targeted, misconfigured, or abused.

AI, therefore, expands the attack surface rather than eliminating traditional security concerns. Protecting intelligent systems requires the same foundational practices used for other critical software: secure design, access controls, monitoring, regular updates, and clear incident-response plans. As AI becomes more integrated into sensitive workflows, treating security as a core component of safety becomes essential.

Responsible AI Frameworks

In response to these concerns, organisations and institutions are developing responsible AI frameworks, which are sets of principles intended to guide the design and deployment of AI systems.

While terminology varies, most ethical frameworks converge around a shared set of core principles:

- *Fairness*—minimising bias and unequal outcomes
- *Transparency*—making systems understandable and explainable where possible
- *Accountability*—assigning clear human responsibility
- *Privacy*—respecting and protecting personal data
- *Human oversight*—ensuring meaningful human involvement in critical decisions

Responsible AI is not only technical; it is organisational and cultural. It involves training teams, setting incentives, and embedding ethical reflection into everyday workflows. Ethics cannot be bolted on after deployment. It must be woven into how systems are imagined, built, evaluated, and governed.

> *Responsibility cannot be automated.*

The New Social Contract

At its core, the ethics of AI is not about machines—it is about people. Every major technological shift has reshaped the implicit agreements between individuals, institutions, and society. AI is no different. As intelligent systems become more capable, society must renegotiate expectations around work, decision-making, responsibility, and trust.

The emerging social contract asks new questions:

- When is it appropriate to delegate decisions to machines?
- What decisions must always remain human?
- How do we balance efficiency with dignity?
- Who benefits, and who bears the risks?

There are no simple answers. But avoiding the conversation is itself a choice—with consequences. The future of AI will not be defined solely by what technology can do; it will be shaped by how consciously humans choose to design, use, and govern intelligent systems. Ethics, regulation, and responsibility are not constraints on progress. They are what make progress worth pursuing.

* * *

Artificial intelligence places new demands on society not because it possesses intent or awareness, but because it magnifies the impact of human choices. As machines grow more capable, the burden of wisdom grows heavier—not lighter.

The most important question is not whether AI can act intelligently, but whether humanity can act responsibly in response to its growing influence.

32

Where AI Is Going and How to Prepare

Every major technological shift ends the same way: not with certainty, but with choice.

Artificial intelligence will continue to advance. Systems will become more capable, more integrated, and more present in everyday life. What remains uncertain is not whether AI will progress, but how humans will respond—as individuals, organisations, and societies.

This final chapter looks ahead without speculation or fear. It focuses on what is likely in the near term, what remains unresolved in the long term, and how preparation—not prediction—is the most reliable response to uncertainty.

The Short-Term Future: More Capability, More Integration

In the near future, AI will not arrive as a single dramatic event. It will continue to spread quietly, unevenly, and incrementally.

Models will improve in context handling, reliability within narrow domains, and deployment speed and cost.

AI will increasingly be embedded in tools people already use, such as writing software, design platforms, search engines, customer systems, and internal business workflows. In many cases, users will not explicitly use AI, but they will benefit from systems that feel more responsive and adaptive. At the same time, familiar limitations will persist. AI will still require human oversight. It will still produce confident errors. It will still reflect the assumptions and constraints of its training data.

AGI: Hype vs. Reality

Earlier, AGI was described as a hypothetical form of AI intended to operate across multiple domains rather than a single task.

Today's AI tools are powerful but specialised. Each is designed for a limited range of tasks, such as writing text, recognising images, or analysing data. These systems do not understand what they are doing, have no goals of their own, and do not learn through real-world experience. They follow patterns in data rather than reasoning about the world as humans do. As a result, advances in AI capability do not necessarily bring progress toward human-like intelligence or consciousness.

Performance improvements often look dramatic, but they remain within the boundaries of task-focused tools. Public discussions sometimes blur this distinction, interpreting each breakthrough as a step toward independent or self-directed machines. In reality, current AI systems remain tools—powerful, useful, and impressive, but entirely dependent on human direction. For this reason, AGI is best understood as a *long-term research idea*, not a near-term reality. While it can be useful for thinking about distant possibilities, it is not a practical guide for today's decisions.

Focusing too heavily on speculative futures can distract from more immediate challenges, such as how AI is applied, where boundaries are drawn, how risks are addressed, and how benefits are shared responsibly.

Preparing for the future does not depend on certainty about AGI; it depends on clarity about human responsibility and how people choose to design, govern, and use the intelligent tools already shaping the world.

Preparing as an Individual

For individuals, preparation is not about becoming an AI expert. It is about developing judgement.

The most resilient individuals in the age of AI will:

- understand what AI is good at and where it fails
- treat AI as a collaborator, not an authority
- verify important outputs rather than accepting them at face value
- remain curious and adaptable as tools evolve

Equally important are skills that are difficult to automate, such as critical thinking, ethical reasoning, communication, creativity, and self-direction. As AI handles more routine tasks, human value increasingly lies in framing problems, asking better questions, and making meaningful decisions.

Preparing as an individual is ultimately about *agency*—using intelligent tools without surrendering responsibility for outcomes.

Preparing as a Business

For organisations, AI preparation is less about technology and more about governance and culture.

Successful businesses align AI with clear goals, apply automation where appropriate, invest in employee training, and embed ethics and accountability into decision-making processes.

AI adoption without clarity creates risk. AI adoption with intention creates leverage. Rather than asking *"What can AI replace?"*, the better question is *"Where can AI responsibly support human work?"*

Businesses that approach AI thoughtfully will not only be more efficient but also more trusted.

Preparing as a Society

At the societal level, preparation is about balance. Societies must encourage innovation while protecting fundamental rights. They must adapt education systems, labour frameworks, and legal structures without freezing progress or abandoning accountability. This requires:

- clear regulatory principles that scale with impact
- transparency about high-risk AI uses
- public literacy about what AI can and cannot do
- shared responsibility across governments, companies, and citizens

The challenge is not technological; it is institutional and ethical. Each society will shape AI according to its own values and priorities. The goal is not uniformity, but deliberate choice rather than passive drift.

A Final Reflection

AI does not determine the future. People do.

The tools we build reflect our assumptions. The systems we deploy amplify our values. The choices we make—about design, governance, and use—will shape outcomes far more than algorithms ever will.

The continued growth of AI capability is no longer in question; its progression appears inevitable. What remains uncertain is whether humanity will act thoughtfully, responsibly, and wisely as AI capabilities expand. The future of AI is therefore not something that unfolds on its own, but something shaped deliberately through human choices.

A Final Thought

> *Capability can be automated; responsibility cannot.*

VI

PART 6—Practical Extras

Part 6 is your toolkit—packed with a glossary, prompts, mini projects, and practical resources you can return to anytime. These extras make the ideas in this book easier to apply, helping you learn faster, work smarter, and build real confidence with AI. Keep this section close; it is designed to support you long after you finish reading.

AI Glossary

Artificial Intelligence (AI)

A broad term for computer systems designed to perform tasks that typically require human intelligence, such as recognising patterns, understanding language, or making predictions.

Algorithm

A set of step-by-step instructions that a computer follows to solve a problem or complete a task.

Bias (in AI)

Consistent tendencies in AI output that favour particular outcomes, viewpoints, or groups, typically arising from skewed or incomplete training data.

Chatbot

An AI-powered system designed to interact with people through conversation, usually by text or voice.

Cognitive Offloading

The practice of using tools or systems to handle mental tasks that would otherwise be performed by the human mind, such as remembering, calculating, or organising information.

Data

Information used by AI systems to learn patterns, make predictions, or generate responses. Data may include text, images, numbers, audio, or video.

Deep Learning

A subset of machine learning that uses multi-layered neural networks to learn complex patterns from large amounts of data.

Embedding

A numerical representation of meaning that allows AI systems to compare and relate words, sentences, or documents based on similarity rather than exact matches.

Fine-Tuning

A process in which a pre-trained AI model is further adjusted using additional data to improve performance for a specific task or domain.

Generative AI

AI systems that are designed to produce new content, such as text, images, music, or code, based on patterns learned from existing data.

Hallucination (in AI)

A situation where an AI system generates information that sounds plausible but is incorrect, fabricated, or unsupported by evidence.

Large Language Model (LLM)

A type of AI model trained on vast amounts of text to understand and generate human-like language.

Machine Learning (ML)

A branch of AI in which systems learn patterns from data rather than being explicitly programmed with fixed rules.

Model

A trained AI system that processes inputs and produces outputs based on learned patterns.

No-Code Platform

A software platform that allows users to build applications or workflows using visual tools and configuration instead of programming.

Prompt

The input or instruction given to an AI system to guide its response or behaviour.

Reinforcement Learning

A learning approach where an AI system improves through feedback, rewards, or penalties based on its actions.

Retrieval-Augmented Generation (RAG)

A technique where an AI system retrieves relevant information from external sources and uses it as context when generating responses.

Token

A unit of text, such as a word or part of a word, that an AI model processes internally.

Training

The process of teaching an AI model by exposing it to data so it can learn patterns and relationships.

Transparency

The extent to which humans can understand the behaviour, limitations, and decision-making processes of an AI system.

Vector Database

A specialised database designed to store and search embeddings, enabling similarity-based retrieval rather than exact matching.

Workflow

A sequence of steps or actions that an AI system or application follows to complete a task.

Artificial General Intelligence (AGI)

A hypothetical concept that describes an AI system capable of operating across multiple domains rather than performing a single task.

Artificial Superintelligence (ASI)

A hypothetical form of AI that would surpass the best human performance across nearly all cognitive domains, including scientific reasoning, creativity, strategic thinking, and social understanding.

Human Oversight

The practice of keeping humans responsible for reviewing, validating, and making final decisions when AI systems are involved.

* * *

This glossary is intended as a practical reference rather than a technical specification. As AI continues to evolve, terms may expand or shift in meaning, but the underlying principles remain grounded in human responsibility, clarity, and intent.

10 Mini Projects

The following mini projects are designed to turn understanding into experience. None require programming skills, and all can be completed using commonly available AI tools or no-code platforms. The goal is not technical perfection, but rather learning how AI behaves, where it is beneficial, and where human judgement remains essential.

1. A Personal AI Study Assistant

Use an AI tool to help explain a topic you are learning. Ask it to summarise concepts, create study questions, or explain ideas in simpler terms. Compare its explanations with trusted sources to practise verification and critical thinking.

What This Teaches:

How AI supports learning without replacing understanding.

2. A Document Summariser for Public Text

Paste a publicly available article, guide, or policy into an AI tool and ask for a clear summary. Experiment with different prompts to see how framing affects the result.

What This Teaches:

How prompts influence output and why context matters.

3. A Writing Companion for Drafting

Ask AI to help draft an email, blog post, or outline based on your ideas. Revise the output yourself to improve tone, accuracy, and clarity.

What This Teaches:

Human–AI collaboration rather than delegation.

4. A Question-and-Answer Assistant for Documents

Provide a small set of non-sensitive documents, such as FAQs or public manuals, and ask the AI to answer questions using only that material. Notice when the system struggles or invents answers.

What This Teaches:

Grounding, hallucination awareness, and safe constraints.

5. A Meeting Notes Organiser

Feed AI a rough set of meeting notes or bullet points and ask it to organise them into clear action items and summaries.

What This Teaches:

Pattern recognition and structure generation.

6. A Decision-Comparison Helper

Present an AI with two or three options for a decision, such as choosing a tool or planning a trip. Ask it to list pros and cons, then evaluate its reasoning yourself.

What This Teaches:

Where AI assists thinking and where judgement must stay human.

7. A Creative Idea Generator

Ask AI to generate ideas for a story, presentation theme, or product concept. Use the results as inspiration rather than final answers.

What This Teaches:

Creativity as collaboration, not automation.

8. A Bias-Detection Exercise

Ask the same question multiple times with slightly different wording. Compare the answers to identify assumptions, framing effects, or missing perspectives.

What This Teaches:

How bias enters outputs and how to recognise it.

9. A Simple No-Code AI Workflow

Using a no-code platform, create a basic workflow that takes user input, sends it to an AI step, and displays the response. Keep the task simple, such as summarising text or answering predefined questions.

What This Teaches:

Systems thinking and AI integration without programming.

10. A Responsible Use Checklist

Design your own checklist for using AI responsibly. Include questions like:

- Is this information sensitive?
- Does this output need verification?
- Who is accountable for the final decision?

What This Teaches:

Ethics, governance, and long-term thinking.

* * *

These projects are intentionally small. Their value lies not in complexity, but in awareness. By experimenting thoughtfully, you learn how AI behaves in practice, where it adds value, and where human responsibility remains essential.

AI literacy grows not through theory alone, but through careful, reflective use.

35 Essential AI Prompts for Daily Use

These prompts are designed to help you communicate clearly with AI, guide its behaviour, and produce useful, grounded results. They emphasise clarity, verification, and collaboration rather than blind delegation.

Thinking and Understanding

1. Explain this concept in simple terms, using a real-world analogy.
2. Summarise this text in three key ideas without adding new information.
3. What assumptions might be hidden in this explanation?
4. What would someone unfamiliar with this topic likely misunderstand?
5. Explain this from multiple perspectives, highlighting where they differ.

Learning and Study

1. Teach this topic step by step, checking understanding at each stage.
2. Create practice questions to test comprehension of this material.
3. Explain this as if I were a beginner, then as if I were more advanced.
4. What background knowledge would help me understand this better?
5. Identify key terms I should look up before continuing.

Writing and Communication

1. Rewrite this for clarity while preserving the original meaning.
2. Improve the structure and flow of this text without changing its tone.
3. Draft a professional version of this message.

4. Suggest alternative phrasings for this sentence.
5. Summarise this content for a general audience.

Planning and Organisation

1. Help organise these ideas into a logical outline.
2. Break this goal into clear, actionable steps.
3. What are the key risks or constraints I should consider?
4. Create a checklist to support consistent decision-making.
5. What information is missing that would improve this plan?

Creativity and Ideation

1. Generate multiple ideas, then explain the strengths of each.
2. Offer creative alternatives that approach this problem from different angles.
3. Combine these two ideas into a coherent concept.
4. Suggest variations that challenge the original approach.
5. What unconventional perspectives could apply here?

Decision Support and Evaluation

1. List pros and cons without recommending a final choice.
2. What trade-offs are involved in each option?
3. What factors should weigh most heavily in this decision?
4. Identify potential unintended consequences.
5. What questions should I ask before deciding?

Verification, Safety and Responsibility

1. What parts of this response should be verified independently?
2. Where might this answer be incomplete or uncertain?
3. Re-evaluate your response and identify possible errors.

4. Limit your answer strictly to the information provided.
5. Explain what you do not know or cannot determine from this input.

Bonus Prompt: A Comprehensive Role-Based AI Prompt

> Act as a thoughtful analytical assistant that supports human decision-making rather than replacing it.
>
> When responding:
> - Clarify assumptions before proceeding
> - Explain your reasoning step by step when appropriate
> - Highlight uncertainty, limitations, or missing information
> - Avoid speculation unless explicitly requested
> - Offer multiple perspectives where relevant
> - Identify potential risks, biases, or ethical considerations
> - Separate facts from interpretations
> - Suggest follow-up questions or verification steps
>
> Your goal is to enhance clarity, understanding, and judgement, ensuring that final decisions remain firmly in human hands.

* * *

Advanced users often take an extra step by asking AI to review or refine a prompt before using it. This helps clarify intent, surface assumptions, and reduce ambiguity before the task begins.

Example:

> "Review this prompt for clarity, hidden assumptions, and potential risks before it is used."

Effective prompting is not about tricking AI into better answers. It is about *clear thinking*, *clear intent*, and *clear boundaries.* The most powerful prompts reflect human judgement, curiosity, and responsibility.

Used well, these prompts turn AI from a passive tool into an active thinking partner—without surrendering control.

AI Tools Directory

This directory is a starting point for exploration rather than a definitive list. AI tools evolve rapidly, with new platforms appearing constantly. Instead of focusing on specific brands, it highlights tool categories, their purposes, and principles for choosing them responsibly.

Readers are encouraged to evaluate tools based on their needs, privacy requirements, and the level of human oversight they require.

Conversational AI and Assistants

Tools in this category enable natural language interaction for tasks such as writing, learning, planning, and problem-solving. They are often used as thinking partners rather than automation engines.

Common uses:

- Drafting and revising text
- Explaining concepts
- Brainstorming ideas
- Answering general questions

What to Consider:

Accuracy, hallucination risk, data handling policies, and the need for verification.

Writing and Content Support Tools

These tools specifically help users write more clearly and efficiently. They may assist with grammar, structure, tone, or summarisation.

Common uses:

- Editing and proofreading
- Improving clarity and flow
- Rewriting for different audiences

What to Consider:

Preserving original intent, avoiding over-reliance, and maintaining a personal voice.

Data Analysis and Spreadsheet Assistants

AI-powered tools in this category help analyse data, generate formulas, clean datasets, and extract insights without advanced technical skills.

Common uses:

- Exploring datasets
- Creating summaries and visual insights
- Generating spreadsheet formulas

What to Consider:

Data sensitivity, results correctness, and the need for human validation.

Software Development Assistants

These tools support developers by suggesting code, explaining errors, generating documentation, or assisting with debugging.

Common uses:

- Code completion and suggestions
- Debugging assistance
- Documentation generation

What to Consider:

Security, correctness, licensing implications, and the need for code review.

No-Code and Low-Code AI Platforms

Platforms in this category allow users to build AI-powered workflows and applications using visual interfaces rather than programming.

Common uses:

- Automating workflows
- Building simple AI-powered tools
- Connecting AI to forms, documents, or databases

What to Consider:

Data isolation, access controls, scalability, and long-term maintainability.

Image, Audio and Creative AI Tools

These tools generate or transform images, audio, video, and other creative assets.

Common uses:

- Visual design and illustration
- Music and audio generation
- Creative experimentation

What to Consider:

Copyright, ethical use, originality, and attribution.

Search, Retrieval and Knowledge Tools

These systems focus on finding, comparing, and retrieving information based on meaning rather than exact keywords.

Common uses:

- Document search
- Knowledge assistants
- Research support

What to Consider:

Source reliability, bias, and whether results are grounded in trusted material.

Choosing Tools Responsibly

When evaluating any AI tool, consider the following questions:

- What problem does this tool actually solve?
- What data does it process, and where is that data stored?
- Does the output require verification?
- Who remains accountable for decisions made using this tool?

The most effective tools are those that augment human capability without removing human responsibility.

* * *

This directory is intentionally non-exhaustive. While AI tools continue to evolve, the principles guiding their responsible selection and use remain unchanged. New tools should be explored with curiosity, care, and clear intent.

Acknowledgements and Resources

No book is written in isolation. Although this work reflects a single voice, it has been shaped by many influences, conversations, and sources of inspiration over time.

First and foremost, thank you to the readers. Curiosity, thoughtful questioning, and a willingness to engage deeply with complex ideas are what make a book like this worthwhile. If this work has helped you see artificial intelligence more clearly, ask better questions, or approach new tools with confidence and care, then it has fulfilled its purpose.

Gratitude is also due to the broader communities of educators, researchers, engineers, writers, designers, and ethicists whose work continues to shape how artificial intelligence is understood and applied. Their efforts to explain, challenge, and responsibly develop these systems form the foundation on which meaningful public understanding can grow.

Special acknowledgement goes to those working to make technology more accessible—through clear writing, open discussion, visual explanation, and patient teaching. In a field often dominated by technical language, clarity is an act of generosity.

Resources for Further Exploration

This book is intended as a starting point rather than a final destination. Readers who wish to continue learning may find value in exploring:

- Introductory materials on artificial intelligence, machine learning, and data literacy
- Writing and research on technology ethics, governance, and responsible innovation
- Public lectures, essays, and interviews from practitioners across disciplines
- Open educational resources that explain AI concepts in an accessible language

Rather than prescribing specific sources, readers are encouraged to seek materials that prioritise clarity, evidence, and thoughtful discussion over hype or speculation.

* * *

Artificial intelligence will continue to evolve, but understanding it is not about keeping pace with every new capability. It is about developing the habits of thinking that allow humans to use powerful tools wisely.

Curiosity, responsibility, and reflection matter more than prediction. Questions matter more than answers, and human values matter more than any system we build.

Thank you for reading.

www.ingramcontent.com/pod-product-compliance
Lightning Source LLC
LaVergne TN
LVHW022201200926
848481LV00006B/1812